Contemporary Art

Klaus Honnef

CONTEMPORARY ART

Benedikt Taschen

Front cover:
Eric Fischl:
Detail from: Bad Boy, 1981
Oil on canvas,
66 ⅛ × 96 in.
(167,6 × 243,8 cm)
Courtesy Mary Boone Gallery, New York

Back cover:
Martin Kippenberger
Sozialkistentransporter, 1989
Wood, paint, plastics,
63 × 220 × 52 ½ in.
(160 × 560 × 134 cm)
Galerie Max Hetzler, Cologne

Frontispiece:
Jeff Koons:
Ushering the Banality, 1988
Wood, 39⅜ × 29 ½ × 64⅞ in.
(100 × 75 × 165 cm)
Galerie Max Hetzler, Cologne

© 1992 Benedikt Taschen Verlag GmbH,
Hohenzollernring 53, D-5000 Köln 1
© 1988 for the illustrations lies with the artists, except:
VG Bild-Kunst, Bonn: Beuys, Warhol
Editor of the illustrations and the appendix: Gabriele Honnef-Harling.
Photographs of the artists: Benjamin Katz, Cologne, except for the following portraits:
Eric Fischl: © Volker Hinz / art; Cindy Sherman: Wilhelm
Schürmann; Basquiat: Janet Montgomery, New York;
Paladino: G. Gorgoni; Longo: Frank Ockenfels.
English translation: Hugh Beyer
Typesetting: Utesch Satztechnik GmbH, Hamburg
Montage: artcolor Verlagsservice, Hamm
Colour reproduction: Repro Color, Bocholt
Printing: Druckerei Ernst Uhl, Radolfzell
Printed in Germany
ISBN 3-8228-0075-9
GB

Contents

Preface

This book is unfair. Because it examines its topic – contemporary art – from only one particular, one-sided point of view. Unfair also in that the chosen perspective does not even do full justice to each of the works that are discussed. It focuses mainly on those artists whose work (in the author's opinion) is representative of a certain change within contemporary art, and it is this change which this book sets out to describe. This means that other artists who have been equally important and influential are often unjustifiably neglected. The author has even disregarded a number of artists whom he values especially, sometimes more than those whose works he has chosen to discuss. And he readily admits that he has put considerably more emphasis on contemporary West German art than on art in France, Holland, Britain, Austria and Switzerland. He has done so from the conviction that within the last fifteen years artistic talent has developed far more in West Germany than in any other country. Not even the U.S.A. could keep up.

The book attempts to describe the state of art today. It concentrates not only on the art world, but also – wherever it seemed necessary – on more general events and tendencies in society and culture as a whole. In particular, it directs the reader's attention to changes within the cultural sphere, the price explosion, the rapid proliferation of art galleries, the museum boom, and the fairy-tale success of a number of individual artists. The aim is to explain some of these phenomena in terms of the specific forms of contemporary art. More emphasis is therefore placed on defining artists' attitudes than on analysing significant works. The author is of course convinced that great works have been created in recent years, but he cannot even try to do justice to all of them.

This book proposes that towards the end of the 20th century there has been quite a considerable and profound change in artistic development. The most important result of this change is that the avant-garde has become historical. The two most prominent artists who paved the way for this seemingly paradoxical change from the avant-garde to the "post-avant-garde" were Andy Warhol and Joseph Beuys. The aesthetic discussion in this book therefore begins with their work. However, this does not mean that the author wishes to herald a new style after the avant-garde – on the contrary: the present situation is so pluralistic that it sometimes verges on randomness. And although the term "post-avant-garde" may sound somewhat dubious, it will nevertheless serve as a valid temporary label, for want of a better term, to summarize all the disparate elements that make up present-day art. What the author definitely wishes to avoid is the false impression that today's art is proceeding along certain well-defined lines. This is by no means the case, and the definition of something that is still in a state of flux has inevitably posed considerable difficulties.

Finally, it is my duty and pleasure to express my thanks to all those who helped with this book – artists and art dealers, as well as private and public collectors who have provided a wealth of illustrations and a lot of valuable advice. I should also like to thank the publishing house, who put so much effort and enthusiasm into the work, particularly Gabriele Honnef-Harling, who tackled the documentary side of the work with an amazing amount of energy, acted as picture editor and wrote the brief biographical notes on the various artists. Also, I should like to express my gratitude to my colleagues at the Rheinisches Landesmuseum in Bonn, Barbara Kückels and Dr. Gail Kirkpatrick, who, together with Gabriele Honnef-

Werner Büttner:
Take Care of Your Teeth like Your Weapons, 1986
Pflege Deine Zähne wie Deine Waffen
Oil on canvas, 74¾ × 59 in.
(190 × 150 cm)
Private collection, Cologne

Harling, all carefully studied the manuscript and made a number of valuable critical comments, as well as to Marion Eckart for patiently preparing the manuscript for printing.

Klaus Honnef

May 1990

The publishers wish to thank Barbara Kückels, Dr. Gail Kirkpatrick, Wilhelm Schürmann, the numerous people who do not wish to be named, the artists, the public collections, the private collectors and, in particular, the gallery owners for permission to reproduce works and for their generous support with photographic material.

Where it was possible to establish the whereabouts and owners of works, these are stated in the captions. Where this was not possible, the gallery which represents the artist is given; in most cases the galleries provided photos for reproduction, even if they no longer own the work of art. The publishers would also like to thank the following photographers: Georg Baselitz; Fotoatelier H. Bernhard, Hardheim; Andreas Brüning, Düsseldorf; Ivan Dalla Tana; D. James Dee; J. Fingerling; Gianfranco Gorgoni; Werner J. Hannappel; Jutta Henselein; Volker Hinz; Bruno Hubschmid, Zurich; Eeva Inkeri; Benjamin Katz, Cologne; J. Littkemann, Berlin; Samuel Marx, Berlin; Frank Mihm, Kassel; André Morain; Ann Münchow, Aachen; Walter Müller; Janet Montgomery, New York; Beth Phillips; Adam Reich, New York; David Reynolds; Ludwig Rinn; Rainer Rosenow, Cologne; Friedrich Rosenstiel, Cologne; Thomas Ruff, Düsseldorf; Bernhard Schaub, Cologne; Lothar Schnepf, Cologne; Philipp Schönborn, Munich (p. 92); Wilhelm Schürmann, Herzogenrath; Steven Sloman, New York; Nic Tenwiggenhorn; Jareth Winters, London; Dorothy Zeidman.

Ashley Bickerton:
Tormented Self-portrait
(Susie at Arles) #2, 1988
Mixed media construction,
90 × 69 × 18 in.
(228.6 × 175.26 × 45.72 cm)
Sonnabend Gallery, New York

The New No Longer New: Zeitgeist

Art has changed over the last few decades. Although continual change is the very essence of art, this change has been running far more deeply, and goes beyond external appearances. The very concept of art is in fact being questioned. At first glance it might indeed seem to be mainly a matter of ephemeral and non-essential questions. For instance, contemporary art has never before enjoyed such wide popularity. Prices are soaring, and private collectors are currently placing an unprecedented number of orders. The boom has been going on for some time now, and the upward trend is continuing. Museums and galleries can hardly accommodate the crowds that appear at the opening of their exhibitions. The prices for modern classics at auctions in London and New York have reached unimaginable heights, as art is increasingly regarded as a sound investment for the future. A Japanese insurance company, for example, paid £24.3 million for Vincent van Gogh's *Sunflowers* – a popular theme but not rare in the oeuvre of this Dutch painter, who only sold one painting in his entire lifetime. Observers of the art business unanimously agreed that this all-time record price for a modern work of art would soon be beaten. They were right. That same year, in November 1987, the record was indeed broken at Sotheby's, where van Gogh's *Fleurs de lis* was sold for the new record of £30.5 million. This indicates how much confidence there is in the future prospects of the art business. And the record price for the Dutch painter was not simply a one-off occurrence. If private investors are prepared to spend such enormous sums of money on painters who died less than a hundred years ago, then they must be extremely optimistic about the future and are expecting new 'van Goghs' to appear. Today's living artists benefit from this attitude both directly and indirectly.

Contemporary art has in fact become an integral part of today's middle-class society. Even works of art which are fresh from the studio are met with enthusiasm. They receive recognition rather quickly – too quickly for the taste of the surlier culture critics. Of course, not all works of art are bought immediately, but there is undoubtedly an increasing number of people who enjoy buying brand new works of art. Instead of fast and expensive cars they buy the paintings, sculptures and photographic works of young artists. They know that contemporary art also adds to their social prestige. Furthermore, since art is not exposed to the same wear and tear as automobiles, it is – in principle – a far better investment. Europe is becoming more and more like America, and in order to be counted among the social élite – or those who think they are the élite – one has to be able to hold one's own in discussions on art. In the Western world, contemporary art enjoys both prestige and the goodwill of politicians. A socialist minister of education in France did more for contemporary art than any of his predecessors, and he became the most popular member of his government. Although he was unable to prevent the defeat of his party at the following parliamentary election, he managed to bring about a major shift in the French cultural scene. In West Germany a conservative head of government willingly allowed contemporary art into the inner sanctum of his office and did not hesitate to promote it by means of extravagant inaugural exhibitions at various museums. State and local authorities in West Germany, towns, provinces and regions in France, Italy and Holland as well as private patrons in the U.K. are constantly vying with one another in founding new museums and art associations. In fact, the planning of new museums has become a sought-after and very attractive job for architects.

A.R. Penck:
Untitled, 1966
Oil on canvas, 51⅛ × 43¼ in.
(130 × 100 cm)
Galerie Michael Werner, Cologne

Page 10:

Georg Baselitz:
Forward Wind, 1966
Vorwärts Wind
Oil on canvas, 63¾ × 51⅛ in.
(162 × 130 cm)
Private collection

Andy Warhol:
Do It Yourself (Seascape), 1962
Acrylic on canvas, 54⅜ × 72 in.
(138 × 183 cm)
Marx Collection, Berlin

A.R. Penck:
Incident in N.Y. 3, 1983
Ereignis in N.Y. 3
Synthetic resin on canvas,
102⅜ × 137¼ in. (260 × 350 cm)
Galerie Michael Werner, Cologne

What immediately strikes us when looking at the various artistic movements of the eighties is that the adjective *new* is used rather liberally. People speak of the *Neue Wilde* (New Savages, Neo-Expressionists), *Neo-Figurative* art, of *new German* and *new Austrian* art. Everything is judged in terms of its "newness". The *Neue Wilde* were soon succeeded by an artistic trend with a neo-geometric programme, called *Neo-Geo*. And that was not the end of it. No sooner had neo-figurative artists and Neo-Geometricians vacated their trend-setting galleries in New York, Cologne, Paris, Vienna, London and Milan to embark on lengthy exhibition tours through international museums, but people's attention was claimed by the *Neo-Conceptualists*. Movements that are launched in spring are often obsolete by the autumn. Oddly enough, it is often the art critics who complain most loudly when there is nothing "new". Yet they are the ones who most strongly oppose the whole direction of contemporary art, resenting the artists' apparent lack of resistance, their obedience to the laws of fashion and the fact that young artists can be as successful at a relatively early stage in their career as if they were stars in the world of show business. Above all, they resent the fact that contemporary art is not looking for the new simply for the sake of newness. Indeed, the inflationary use of the word *new* in connection with artistic trends does not correspond at all to current terminology. It never actually appears on its own but only ever as a prefix *(Neo-)* or as an adjective qualifying a trend which already exists. New tendencies are not really all that new, nor are they meant to be. This tends to make it easy for art critics to deride art, claiming that all the hollow talk about "new" art merely serves to disguise the emperor's nakedness.

Andersen's tale of the emperor's new clothes has accompanied modern art from the very beginning. People have always enjoyed ridiculing artistic tendencies that were genuinely new. But the terms of abuse which they used have now become the officially sanctioned

A.R. Penck:
Standpoint, 1971
Standort
Acrylic on canvas, 114⅛ × 114⅛ in.
(290 × 290 cm)
Staatsgalerie, Stuttgart

Page 16:

Martin Disler:
Thinking of India, 1982
Acrylic on canvas, 90½ × 63 in.
(230 × 160 cm)
FER Collection

Karl Horst Hödicke:
Black Gobi, 1982
Schwarze Gobi
Synthetic resin on canvas, 67 × 90½ in.
(170 × 230 cm)
Galerie Gmyrek, Düsseldorf

names which serve to distinguish the various periods and artistic tendencies from one another. Nowadays only historians are aware of the original negative meanings of Baroque, Rococo, Impressionism, Fauvism and Cubism. Since the end of the First World War and the victory of abstract art, such labels have come to reflect the artists' self-image. Some were invented by the artists themselves and some by authors and art critics who could identify with their work. And so they mark an important change of attitudes among the middle classes towards contemporary art. The more enlightened and progressive members of the middle classes realized that – despite its obvious anti-bourgeois overtones – contemporary art had the potential to break out of the cultural fetters of the 19th and 20th centuries.

There was too much of a contradiction between the bourgeois stuffiness of a typical middle-class sitting-room and the world of technology. Quite a few people believed that contemporary art was an accurate reflection of modern civilization, a world marked by rapid technological development, far-reaching political and social revolutions, sudden economic booms as well as disasters. And so the central avant-gardist idea of contemporary art throughout the first two thirds of our century was almost automatically linked to faith in progress within our modern industrial society, though this does not necessarily imply that the artists approved. After all, the bourgeoisie was regarded by them as a rather inferior breed. But that faith in progress which pervaded the whole of society obviously also affected the art world. Art, after all, does not exist in isolation from society. No matter how indignantly individual artists may react to certain phenomena within society, they can only ever react as individuals, whereas their art – if it is art at all – is inevitably subject to the *zeitgeist*.

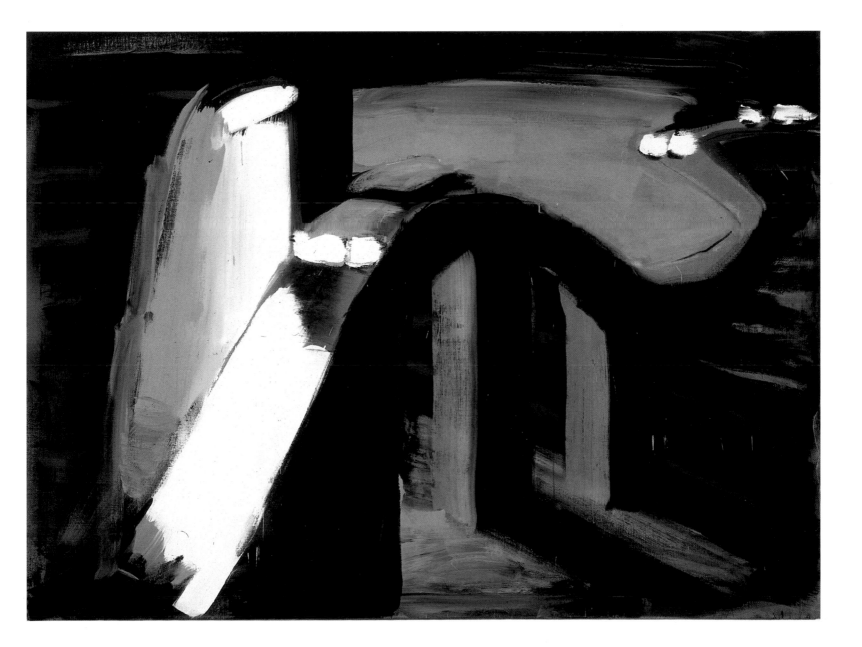

Jörg Immendorff:
And Now the 38th Party Congress:
Café Deutschland, 1983
Auf zum 38. Parteitag:
Café Deutschland
Oil on canvas, 74¾ × 86⅝ in.
(190 × 220 cm)
Galerie Michael Werner, Cologne

Georg Baselitz:
Great Friends, 1965
Die großen Freunde
Oil on canvas, 98½ × 118 in.
(250 × 300 cm)
The 20th Century Museum (Museum
des 20. Jahrhunderts), Ludwig Collection, Vienna

Jiri Georg Dokoupil:
In Search of the Twentieth Century Icon, 1983
Dispersion on muslin, 78¼ × 143¼ in.
(200 × 365 cm)
Private collection, Cologne

Page 20:

Susan Rothenberg:
Untitled, 1979
Acrylic and flashe on paper,
42¼ × 30¼ in. (107.3 × 76.8 cm)
Sperone Westwater Gallery, New York

The twenties and, later, the sixties, saw the culmination of the conflict between bourgeois art and a culturally conservative bourgeoisie. The leading representatives of middle-class society seemed like narrow-minded philistines to the artists, and the various governmental organizations seemed in fact to justify this criticism by the way in which they hit back. This gave rise to the misunderstanding among artists that their work promoted social revolution, and many of them therefore became involved in revolutionary parties and movements. In revolutionary Russia quite a few artists had to pay for this misunderstanding with their lives. After the Second World War the conflict was mainly verbal. Especially in West Germany progressive artists felt the pressure of political and social restoration and saw themselves initially as outsiders. However, the gap was soon closed. The Second World War had literally turned the world upside down and put it back on its feet again. Nothing had remained as before, including culture and art. The ancient traditions were falling apart, and people were beginning to escape from the social conventions which – until then – had been considered paramount. Even a private social institution such as the family was losing its original permanence and stability. It was a development which generally had a rather peculiar effect on contemporary art, because it was now lagging behind artistic positions which people thought belonged to the past. After all, had there not been a strong element of logic in the development of art from various forms of representational paintings and sculptures to the daring designs of abstraction? From the material to the spiritual realm?

It seemed that, with the advent of Pop Art in the sixties, such ideas were abandoned completely. Pop Artists could not have cared less about the noble ideals of abstract art. They used the language of the street, their artistic vocabulary came straight from popular comic strips, and they exploited the photography and films of the mass media. Unlike their illustrious predecessors in art history, they did not pay tribute to the Blessed Virgin Mary or the ancient goddess of love, but to the seductive sirens of Hollywood movies. Partly, however, the desire to shock the bourgeois establishment was still present in Pop Art. After all, abstract art – i.e. Informal Art in Europe and Abstract Expressionism in the U.S. – had lost its progressive power and had turned into a rigid convention. This, above all, was what Pop Artists resented and rebelled against, though still in the name of progress and still obeying the demand that art should reflect everyday life and that everyday life should be found within art.

Markus Lüpertz:
Dithyrambe, 1964
Distemper on muslin, 59 × 59 in.
(150 × 150 cm)
Galerie Michael Werner, Cologne

Page 23:

Per Kirkeby:
Winter VI, 1986
Oil on canvas, 78¼ × 51⅛ in.
(200 × 130 cm)
Galerie Michael Werner, Cologne

From the turn of the century onwards there has been increasing doubt about the idea that the world was progressing towards paradise on earth. Everywhere on this planet there have been cruel and pointless wars, our natural environment is being destroyed at a phenomenal speed by poisonous industrial waste, the amount of traffic has increased like a cancer, and there have been technological disasters of unprecedented, apocalyptic proportions – such as the nuclear catastrophes of Seveso, Bophal and Chernobyl. A third of mankind are suffering from hunger and starvation, while a fifth are living in the lap of luxury, and human beings are becoming increasingly aggressive towards each other. These are only some of the facts which have shaken man's unshakeable faith in progress. Day by day the mass media – itself a product of our technological age – brings news of all these horrors straight into our homes. As a result, people are of course considerably better informed, but at the same time they have become less sensitive and their perception has been blunted. Most people have become used to the continuous threat to their physical existence, and as long as it does not actually affect them personally, they do not feel that it concerns them in any way. A small number of people try to maintain an awareness of the danger in which we find ourselves, but in order to attract any attention at all they must, paradoxically, use the same media which dull people's minds. Therefore many feel that this mechanically and electronically produced reality is a kind of theatrical spectacle which is far more exciting than daily life or art.

Considering that artists are also affected by social conditions, it hardly needs mentioning that even they have lost their faith in the continuous progress of art. In this respect the art critics are indeed right in claiming that the cheap labels for the art of the eighties are nothing but empty talk. But their clever minds have failed to see that their sharp arrows have missed their mark, that they have shot past both the works of art and the way in which the artists see themselves. The over-generous use of the word *new* only obscures the essence. None of the artists under attack really understood the problem and were therefore unable to pay any serious attention to the arguments which were brought forward against them. The intentions that were imputed to them did not match the actual works of art. Often it was the critics themselves who – for want of better terminology – gave them these labels.

The term *Neue Wilde* (New Savages, Neo-Expressionists), for instance, was coined by the museum curator Wolfgang Becker (Aachen, West Germany) in an essay on artists such as Robert Kushner and Kim MacConnel. He then applied the same term to painters such as Georg Baselitz, Markus Lüpertz, A.R. Penck, Anselm Kiefer, because he wanted to suggest that there was a link between the sumptuousness of the American artists, the expressive paintings of the German artists and the Fauve circle around Henri Matisse. It was in fact the old question about the relationship between French Fauvism and German Expressionism around the year 1910. Becker could indeed have opened up an interesting discussion, for his essay did not merely attempt to explain the increase of expressive and representational tendencies in contemporary art, but he also established a link between neo-figurative developments in American and German art as well as their common basis in the European tradition. Unfortunately, however, this discussion never took place. Instead, Becker's undoubtedly disputable new term was applied to artists whose unrestrained activities in the early eighties provided a sudden breath of fresh air in contemporary art, changing its face overnight. This misinterpretation may have been due to the fact that these artists also used a figurative vocabulary. But what is less understandable is the way in which Baselitz, Lüpertz, Penck and Kiefer were immediately hailed as "Fathers of the Neo-Expressionists".

However, what particularly impressed the public was the ferocity and speed at which this abrupt artistic innovation took place. And people were equally amazed that it was not confined to any one particular country, but that it encompassed the entire Western hemisphere. In the United States a number of artists had already been opposing the cool aestheticism of Minimal Art for quite some time and with some degree of success. The situation in Europe was similar. Admittedly, though, these artistic protests went virtually unnoticed by those members of the public who were interested in art. European art at that date was still totally under the spell of the American avant-garde, as manifested in Concept Art, and its effect on paintings.

This was particularly harsh in West Germany, and Baselitz suffered under this, because at the time many believed that they had to make an example of him. Whenever his work was not actually ignored – which happened most of the time – it was branded as an unsuccessful, coarsely painted version of neo-realism. His method of painting motifs upside down was felt

to be cheap showmanship. At best, more favourable critics saw this as an allegory of the state of the world. In Italy, however, someone as enterprising and inventive as Achille Bonito Oliva had formed a powerful lobby together with a number of young painters from different parts of the country. They coined the rather attractive term *trans-avant-garde* for their artistic position. Samples of this artistic trend had reached Germany through several German art dealers. It was by no means coincidental that an exhibition organized by Hans Jürgen Müller in Stuttgart was given the programmatic title *Europe 79*, an exhibition which included all the 'newest' trends.

Those who had eyes saw indeed. The enterprise was sponsored by both private donations and public funds. Although works shown by the galleries were mostly by younger artists, the exhibition signalled a turning point: the Italian contribution, in particular, was full of ostentatious self-confidence. It was obvious that a fresh wind was blowing in Italian art. Although some of these largely unknown artists still betrayed the influence of *arte povera*, which had dominated the Italian scene for a whole decade, the exhibition was not without its unusual aspects, particularly Francesco Clemente's paintings, Sando Chia's picture-object combinations, and Nino Langobardi's spectacular arrangement of a tiger skin nailed to the wall and the floor. Most unusual of all was the obvious return to traditional forms of painting and the subjectivity of the works. The latter was all the more daring and innovative because it contrasted with the conscious emphasis on anonymity in Minimal and Concept Art. While the artists of the Minimalist movement had always stressed the objective truthfulness of art as art

Nino Longobardi:
Untitled, 1986
Mixed media on canvas, 39⅜ × 51½ in.
(100 × 131 cm)
Galerie Bugdahn & Szeimies, Düsseldorf

and had tried to avoid any hint of personal involvement, the artist as an individual now asserted himself in the paintings, sculptures and spatial arrangements of the Italians. Though still hesitantly, the artist was beginning to make his presence known, as was the entire physical and psychological environment in which he moved.

Admittedly, few of the participants actually dared to undermine the demand that avant-garde art should be totally autonomous and independent of its creator. And nobody could have known that within months there would be a revolutionary change in contemporary art, with the triumphant return of representational art. At the same time *Europe 79* was symptomatic in its significance: the exhibition showed a marked increase in self-confidence among European artists and a strong determination to challenge the seemingly omnipotent aestheticism of the right angle and pure abstraction, with paintings that included a new kind of imagination, the emotions of the individual, the subconscious mind, man's sense of the mysterious, and not least his sensuality and seductiveness.

Nino Longobardi:
Untitled, 1979
Installation Europe 79, Stuttgart 1979
Canvas and tiger skin, 78¾ × 196⅞ in.
(200 × 500 cm)
Galerie Bugdahn & Szeimies, Düsseldorf

Between Tradition and Innovation

As soon as we try to identify the causes of this far-reaching change in contemporary art, we find a whole host of reasons within art itself. Not only was there a profound change of general attitudes towards contemporary art in the Western world, but also, at the same time, quite a dramatic change within art itself. Both are closely related. But it is difficult to distinguish clearly between cause and effect. From a structural point of view the development can be seen as a continuous process of action and reaction. An important feature of this change is the almost complete renunciation of aesthetic principles, with the result that the artist no longer feels in strict opposition to society. In practice, this heritage of avant-garde art had eventually amounted to a gesture of permanent rejection. The tautological slogan was "art as a function of art". For the majority of artists such a path had turned into a dead end. At the same time, it was an attitude that reflected the artists' capitulation to society, if they had not been absorbed by it already. There are of course still a considerable number of artists who want to abide by the aims of modernism in their works, but no longer at any price and not in the present form.

It had been the declared aim of the avant-garde that once an artistic position had been reached it should be questioned by means of an interminable chain of innovations, in order to avoid the unrestrained consumption of works of art. By contrast, the post-avant-garde artists show absolutely no fear that their art might be falsely claimed by certain ideological positions. However, when we summarize the dominating tendencies of the eighties as "post-avant-garde", then this should not mean that artists have abandoned avant-garde positions completely. In fact, it is still claimed that works of art should be autonomous. "The concept of art in the age of the bourgeoisie means quite emphatically that art serves no master, that it is autonomous and free from all aims and purposes. It defines its own essence, its claims, its laws, it has a duty to no one except itself and the great abstract principles of mankind in the future and in eternity. Such autonomous art tends towards the esoteric. It precludes elements of entertainment, the joy of looking and listening, and we can therefore identify such things as light music, popular art and cheap rubbish."

What distinguishes post-avant-garde art from the avant-garde is the conscious attempt to break up the hierarchical structures described by the German historian Thomas Nipperdey in the above quotation. The world of commerce and consumption, of the mass media and of popular art is no longer regarded as an opposite pole; instead, artists try to make perfectly deliberate use of it as a welcome source of inspiration – and in fact with the same earnestness that they apply to their own tradition. In contemporary post-avant-garde art the boundaries between these spheres are no longer as clear-cut as they used to be, but rather more fluid, so that the most typical works contain elements of both respectable art and the trite pictures of mass culture. Although many of their artistic strategies are reminiscent of the sixties Pop Art, there are nevertheless enormous differences between the two. Pop Artists repeatedly emphasized that they were aiming, as it were, to lend respectability to the images which they borrowed from mass culture through an artistic revision. With the exception of Andy Warhol, nothing would have been further from their minds than the levelling of the ancient hierarchical relationship between serious art and popular mass culture.

But this is precisely what post-avant-garde artists are aiming to do – an attitude reinforced by their observation that the pictures of mass culture, which have been held so much in

Jeff Koons:
Louis (XIV), 1986
Stainless steel, 45 × 27 × 15 in.
(116.8 × 68.6 × 38.1 cm)
Private collection, New York

Page 26:

Herbert Brandl:
Untitled, 1984/85
Oil on canvas, 70⅞ × 59 in.
(180 × 150 cm)
Private collection, Cologne

Ian McKeever:
Crossing, 1986
Oil on photo canvas, 98½ × 169¼ in.
(250 × 430 cm)
Fredrik Ross Collection, Sweden

contempt, are far more suitable as vehicles for their emotions than the self-contained imageless images of avant-garde art. And there was yet another argument in favour of adopting elements from mass culture. First of all, their widespread use and their high suggestive density give them a certain autonomous status, even though – superficially – this may not always be very obvious. On the other hand, however, the merging of the artistic configuration of high art and popular mass culture has led to subversive images which both sides find somewhat irritating. Thus it is possible for post-avant-garde artists to counter the embraces of society with their own strategies of embracing society. If, until recently, art was the folk-tale hare in its relationship with society, artists of the eighties are now assuming the role of the tortoise, i.e. they are playing the same game in the opposite role.

As artists developed a different understanding of art, their image also changed. Since most of them belong to a generation that grew up with television, they have not only transcended the traditional categories of avant-garde art, but also the narrow confines of each of their specific domains. Just as there are very few dominant styles or even directions in post-avant-garde art, artists do not normally see themselves as art specialists with certain definite trademarks. Hardly any of them specializes exclusively in painting, sculpture, or photography. Rather, it has become typical of their specific art that they now mix the most disparate disciplines, such as painting and photography, photography and performance, painting and sculpture, sculpture and architecture, architecture and design, design and photography. On the whole, post-avant-garde art adds up to a multi-media display which, however, has nothing in common with the *Gesamtkunstwerk* in the age of Romanticism. It is of no consequence that some of their works might have been influenced by popular rock music, which has also tended to incorporate post-avant-garde painting. Nor does it matter whether or not several of them have dabbled with music.

There can be no question that post-avant-garde artists no longer see themselves as social outcasts, but have made a conscious effort to become part of the media world of mass culture. This then is how the middle-class geniuses of the 19th and 20th centuries have become the stars and super-stars of present-day art. And indeed why not? But to say that this vigorous development means the end of art or – worse still – the end of our modern age, is simply and utterly wrong. Robert Hughes, the sharp-witted art critic of the American news magazine *Time*, summed up the situation very aptly: "When one speaks of the end of modernism – and it is no longer possible to avoid doing so, for the idea that we are in a 'post-modernist' culture has been a commonplace since the mid-seventies – one does not invoke a sudden historical terminus. Histories do not break off clean, like a glass rod; they fray, stretch, and come undone like rope. There was no specific year in which the Renaissance ended; but it did end, although culture is still permeated with the active remnants of Renaissance thought. So it is with modernism, only more so, because we are much closer to it. Its reflexes still jerk, the severed limbs twitch, the parts are still there; but they no longer connect or function as a live whole. The modernist achievement will continue to affect culture for another century at least, because it was large, so imposing, and so irrefutably convincing. But its dynamic is gone, and our relationship to it is becoming archaeological. Picasso is no longer a contemporary, or a father figure; he is a remote ancestor, who can inspire admiration but not opposition. The age of the New, like that of Pericles, has ended history."

Susan Rothenberg:
Blue Frontal, 1978
Acrylic, flashe and tempera on canvas,
77 × 88½ in. (195.6 × 224.8 cm)
Sperone Westwater Gallery, New York

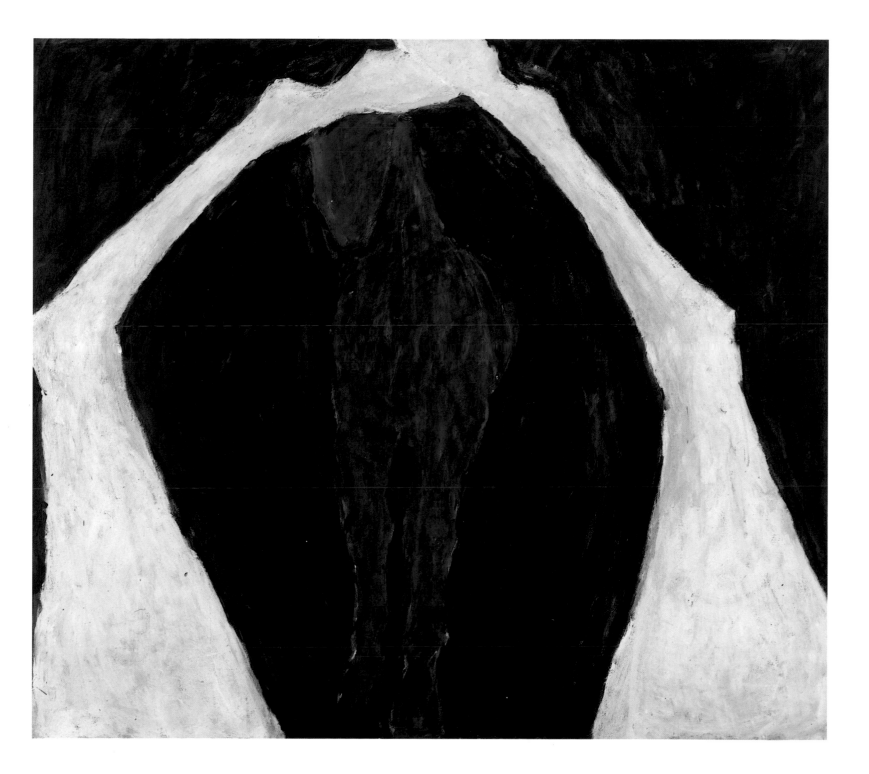

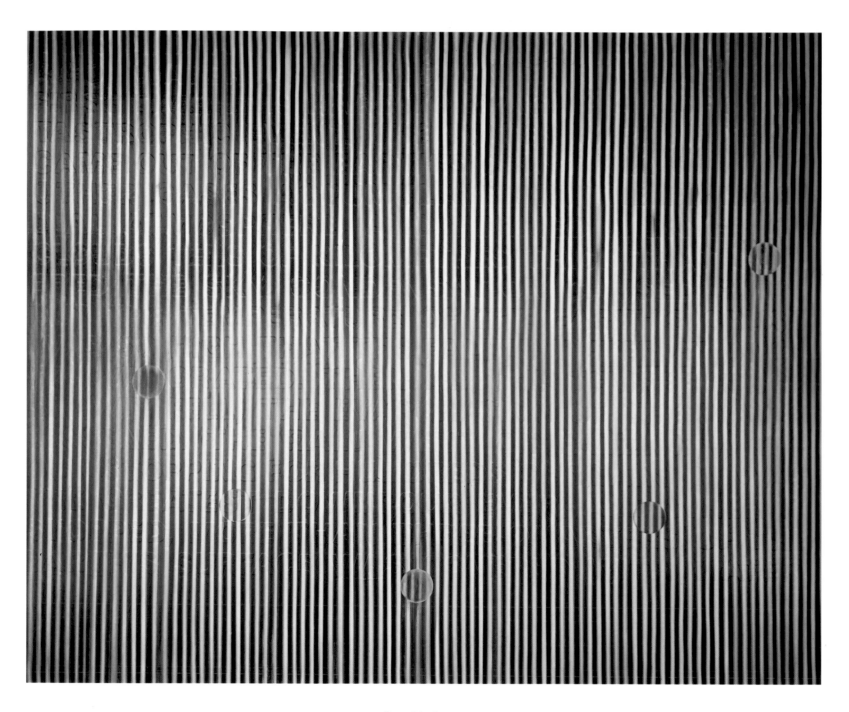

Ross Bleckner:
Oceans, 1984
Oil and wax on canvas, 120 × 144 in.
(304.8 × 365.8 cm)
Emily and Jerry Spiegel Collection,
New York

Keith Haring:
Exhibition from 3rd – 30th May 1984
Galerie Paul Maenz, Cologne

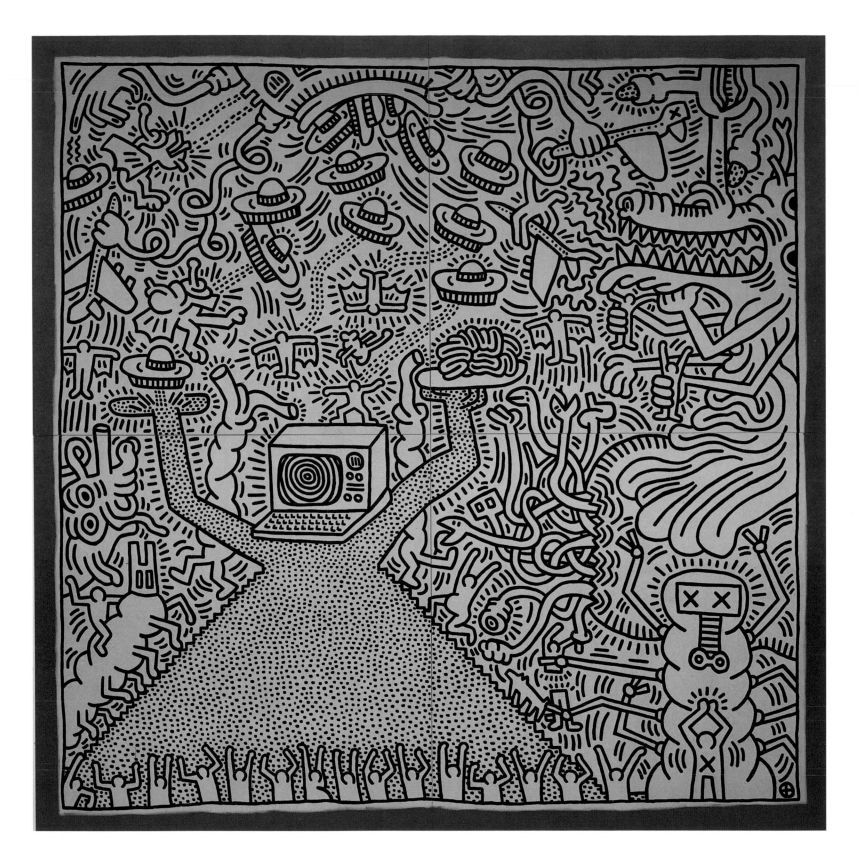

Keith Haring:
Untitled, April 1984
Acrylic on muslin, in four parts,
120 × 120 in. (304 × 304 cm)
Galerie Paul Maenz, Cologne

Keith Haring:
Untitled, 12th April 1984
Acrylic on muslin, 59¾ × 59¾ in.
(152 × 152 cm)
Galerie Kaess-Weiss, Stuttgart

When we consider all the products of artistic imagination created at the end of the seventies and the beginning of the eighties, both in Europe and in the U.S., a number of distinctive features emerge: joy in the unrestrained use of colour and shapes, a wealth of imagination, a feeling for decorative effects and a carelessness towards orthodox artistic conformity, particularly to that of the avant-garde. There is a refreshing lack of system, a certain nonchalance in dealing with seemingly incompatible styles, which sometimes gives the impression of a stylistic hotchpotch. Elements of 'higher art' freely intermingle with 'lesser' forms of art. The artist displays his ego quite demonstratively, sometimes even in an excessively narcissistic and exhibitionistic way. Some works of art radiate an eroticism which is no more confined by convention than the artistic style of the work itself. Playfulness, often verging on the superfluous, exists side by side with shrill cynicism, destructive anger and anarchic zest, but with an underlying sense of profound despair, which is expressed in attitudes ranging from irony to bitter sarcasm. There are outbreaks of hidden romanticism sometimes bordering on the sentimental, as well as a joy in contradiction, even undisguised aggressiveness, and a lack of utopian perspective. The general attitude which sums up all these features can probably best be described as cynicism in the spirit of Diogenes, the 'patriarch of Sinope'. He defined it as the "doggish lack of respect of a lesser theory in league with poverty, satire and insolence, a theory which – in view of the idealistic abstractions and dullness of mere head knowledge and the hollow pompousness of art - tries to piss into the wind of idealism." (Jörg Drews)

"Lack of respect" may indeed be the best way of describing the attitude of post-avant-garde artists: a lack of respect towards any conventions whatever, be they social or artistic in origin, and particularly towards the premises of an aesthetic theory with a strong intellectual bias and therefore a marked deficit in perception. At a time when there was a danger that artists would merely follow in the footsteps of the avant-garde, it was this unorthodox attitude which

Bernd Koberling:
Big Breeder, 1981
Großer Brüter
Synthetic resin and oil on canvas,
74¾ × 106¼ in. (190 × 270 cm)
Galerie Gmyrek, Düsseldorf

enabled them to take a fresher, less biased look at the traditional forms of figurative art than the doctrinaire champions of the avant-garde. In West Germany a number of artists picked up the threads of Expressionism, in Italy and France it was the controversial *Novecento* art which attracted attention, and in the U.S. a number of important artists re-discovered the forgotten sources of authentic folk art, thus emphasizing the cultural autonomy of their multi-national state. It was in the context of this cultural "melting-pot" that the idea of a "post-modern" (Hughes) culture manifested itself. It is one of the most striking features of post-avant-garde art that it expresses cultural differences far more strongly than the artistic movements of the avant-garde, which were largely international. The Italians, for instance, have a distinct preference for classical mythology and its succinct imagery, whereas the Germans tend more towards eccentricity, and the Americans towards playful pragmatism. What all these national characteristics have in common is that they represent a manifold diversity of scintillating aesthetic elements, without the slightest trace of dogmatic rigidity. In addition, there is a strong element of subjectiveness, which must not be overlooked, marked by a tendency to overstate and exaggerate, often with a trace of narcissism and hedonism.

This brief description shows how difficult it is to reduce the artistic scene of the eighties to a common denominator. There are so many differences that it is impossible to measure everything against one yardstick. Furthermore, firm contours only emerge gradually, and there is a good deal of overlap between the individual trends, without clearly defined

Stefan Szczesny:
Bathers in the Snow, 1984
Badende im Schnee
Oil on canvas, 78¾ × 98½ in.
(200 × 250 cm)
Karl Pfefferle Galerie & Edition, Munich

borderlines. The German sociologist Jürgen Habermas has described the social and cultural situation at the end of the 20th century as a "new obscurity" and this also applies to contemporary art. According to Andreas Huyssen, a lecturer in literature in New York, contemporary art is currently in the midst of transition: "Post-Modern art of the eighties is marked by tension between tradition and innovation, conservatism and progressiveness, mass culture and serious culture. However, the latter is no longer given a privileged position over the former, and the old dichotomies and categories no longer function in the same old reliable way, e.g. progress vs reaction, left vs right, rationalism vs the irrational, future vs past, modernism vs realism, abstraction vs representation, avant-garde vs cheap rubbish."

With post-avant-garde trends there has also been a return to exuberant sensuality in the art world. Indeed it is quite symptomatic that there has been a triumphant renaissance of paintings – so triumphant, in fact, that one particular, widely-read book diagnosed a hunger for pictures in its very title *(Hunger nach Bildern)* - at a time when everybody is virtually flooded with visual stimuli. It is said that artists have turned into avid painters, that they have been seized by an obsessive desire to paint. In 1980 Paul Maenz, who had already supported a group of Italian artists called *Transavantguardia*, organized an exhibition called *Mülheimer Freiheit und interessante Bilder aus Deutschland* ("The Freedom of Mülheim and Interesting Paintings from Germany"). It came as a relief and hit the country like a thunderbolt. Gone was the deadly boredom which had paralysed the German art world for so many years, with only occasional interruptions, such as the *Schlaglichter* ("Highlights") exhibition at the Rheinisches Landesmuseum in Bonn, which summarized on a national level what the Stuttgart exhibition *Europe 79* had done on a European scale. It was so obvious that the painters had great pleasure in painting their pictures that this spilled over to the viewers. Even the more critically-minded among them, who were later to adopt a sceptical – if not hostile – attitude towards the entire movement, could not remain impervious to the direct sensual

impact of the paintings. It was irrelevant that the painters had an insufficient grasp of the rules of their craft – indeed many of them really did not know much about painting at all – or that they had flouted the most basic avant-garde rules.

In a way, everything was wrong about the exhibition, whose only programme consisted in the claim that it did not have one. Even the title suggested this. Mülheimer Freiheit *("The Freedom of Mülheim"),* which sounded rather like a catchy brandname, gave the false impression of a sworn community of artists who were following the example of the *Brücke* artists. In reality they were no more than the pragmatic union of a group of painters (Hans Peter Adamski, Peter Bömmels, Walter Dahn, Jiri Georg Dokoupil, Gerard Kever and Gerhard Naschberger) who had managed to rent a large warehouse in a Cologne suburb and were using it as a big studio. The second part of the title ("Interesting Paintings from Germany") simply meant that the exhibition also included a number of other German artists, such as Ina Barfuss, Thomas Wachweger, Werner Büttner, Albert Oehlen and Georg Herold. It is significant that the name Mülheimer Freiheit was abandoned by the artists as soon as it really did come to be regarded as a trademark. Whichever perspective one chose to adopt, this art – which did not yet have a marketable name – refused to add up to an uncontradictory consistent whole. It reminded one of much that was already known. On the other hand, it also illustrated a vivid imagination. Indeed, the sheer joy of painting, joy in the physical process itself, could be seen in the choice of subjects. Many paintings dealt with defecation, vomiting and sexuality. It seemed that this art was inherently contradictory, deliberately provoked confusion. But there was also an element of helpless perplexity in this art, a certain amount of despair. "If we hadn't been successful with these pictures," said Adamski, "then most of us would have given up painting." Adamski was the oldest of the group and the only one who had already made an original contribution to Conceptual Art. His statement expressed neither unrestrained opportunism nor sheer cynicism, but rather the attitude of playful nonchalance which these painters had developed towards painting and a certain aloofness which – because of their experiences as artists – they maintained towards any ideological limitations.

The Maenz exhibition made it quite clear that the *Mülheimer Freiheit* artists had no respect for any of the usual rules of contemporary art, except perhaps the rule that paintings tend to be rectangular. And they continued to keep their distance even when, in the course of the years, they had risen to the height of highly-paid stars of the international art scene. Whatever their paintings were about and irrespective of the artistic attitudes by which they had been influenced, they were no more than the crest of the wave – a wave which was to engulf the entire Western world like a deluge and eventually broke up the strongly defended bastions of a rather rigid concept of the avant-garde.

Andreas Schulze:
Untitled, 1985
Dispersion on muslin, 90½ × 133⅞ in.
(230 × 340 cm)
Galerie Monika Sprüth, Cologne

Martin Kippenberger:
War Wicked,1983
Krieg böse
Oil on canvas, 39⅜ × 47¼ in.
(100 × 120 cm)
Galerie Max Hetzler, Cologne

The Seventies as a Laboratory

Only a very short time separated their death – the German artist from the Lower Rhine and the American artist whose ancestors had come from Czechoslovakia. Both had become more famous than any of their contemporaries. Indeed, they had become legendary long before they died. They embodied two opposite poles, and yet they were as close as two sides of the same coin. They knew each other well, but were not really very close friends. One of them painted a portrait of the other, thus putting his colleague's countenance firmly among the great figures of show business and the art world – a gallery of faces which had become a significant element in the artist's oeuvre. Both were extremely interested in myths. The one would conjure up images of man's primaeval anxieties, while at the same time offering him comfort, the other used to paint the circus-like Olympian world of the media, whose modern "court minstrel" he became. It is difficult to gauge their influence on both sides of the Atlantic, but one cannot help feeling that there is something symbolical about the fact that they both died in the mid-eighties. Joseph Beuys and Andy Warhol were rather an unequal couple to be yoked together, and the positions from which they paved the way for post-avant-garde art were diametrically opposed to each other. Nonetheless, both artists fulfilled the decisive roles of mediators and were, so to speak, the head chemists in that 'laboratory of sorts', which is how the American critic and poet Peter Schjeldahl described the art of the seventies.

Beuys was the first post-war German artist to receive an international reputation. His ideas and artistic strategies, the ingenious way in which he treated the most diverse materials and techniques, his amazing ability to direct the whole host of associations connected to these materials both sensitively and accurately, in order to unleash their potential and to channel them into new lines – this is what gave him his reputation. But none of these qualities explain his worldwide charisma, his simply overwhelming influence on contemporary art. Among artists, Beuys was probably more sensitive than anyone else to the dramatic revolutionary changes which were taking place in the eighties. Although he did not, in principle, question the autonomy of art, he nevertheless filled his works so much with day-to-day reality that they virtually bulged with it and inevitably made an immediate impact on the viewer. Also, the unity of life and work which he practised gave his artistic manifestations a high degree of moral authority. Throughout his life, Beuys would put his finger on the world's open sores – a world which seemed to be getting more and more intangible and which was continually splitting into a multitude of autonomous and incompatible regulative systems far removed from reality. Both as a person and as an artist, Beuys would bring about strong reactions: harsh rejection on the one hand and unconditional, sometimes rapturous enthusiasm on the other.

Beuys's art is an expression of man's broken relationship with reality, although his concept of reality was considerably more complex than that of a self-appointed crisis manager. It encompassed space and time, nature and culture, real life and a concrete utopia. In other words, his idea of reality was very universal. It included not only his entire artistic activities – his sculptures, environments and works on paper, as well as the photographed, filmed and videographed documents of his artistic performances and his numerous written and spoken statements – but in fact every individual piece of art that he had ever created. Each one of

Andy Warhol:
Campbell's Soup Can I, 1968
Acrylic and liquitex on canvas, screenprint,
36 × 24 in. (91.5 × 61 cm)
Neue Galerie, Ludwig Collection, Aachen

Page 40:

Andy Warhol:
Portrait of Joseph Beuys, 1980
Acrylic, liquitex and diamond dust on canvas,
screenprint, 100 × 119⅝ in.
(254 × 203 cm)
Marx Collection, Berlin

Joseph Beuys:
Table with Aggregate, 1958-1985
Tisch mit Aggregat
Bronze and copper, 38¾ × 22⅞ × 66 in.
(98.5 × 58 × 170 cm)
Galerie Schmela, Düsseldorf

Page 43:

Joseph Beuys:
Concert Grand Yom (Area Yom), 1969
Konzertflügeljom (Bereichjom)
on permanent loan to the Städtisches
Kunstmuseum Bonn by Ulbricht

them reflects his universal world view in a nutshell. In the same way it also encapsulates a counter-image to the normal image of reality – which to the ordinary contemporary appears as a conglomerate of unrelated realities with more or less independent characters.

In the ordinary sense of the word, however, neither Beuys's world view nor his art can be called 'realistic'. Does that mean that they have nothing in common with empirical reality after all? On the contrary. Anyone who takes a deeper interest in his work soon realizes that it deals with questions that are highly topical. Basic questions which concern everyone, not 'philosophical' ones in an elevated sense. Beuys would remind people of forgotten or lost interconnections of life, with a visual vocabulary full of metaphors, rich in symbols and extraordinarily sculptural. He would draw these interconnections out of the dungeons of the subconscious into which they had been dropped, and then display them openly in the light of the conscious mind. Nature and civilization, man and technology, past, present and future, art and life were by no means incompatible dimensions for him. He was neither a backward-looking romantic nor an unrealistic utopian, neither a magician nor a charlatan. After his death, his most zealous disciples endeavoured to surround his name with a certain halo and his art with an aura of sacredness. It was a grotesque misunderstanding which prematurely turned his art into museum pieces and robbed it of its impact.

But why was it that Beuys's art provoked so much irritation during his lifetime, why was it so frequently reviled and defamed, and why was the artist himself so much under attack? The answer is relatively simple. Seen against the background of a reality that has dozens of contradictory explanations, it was inevitable that nearly everything the artist thought and did should seem unusual, if not provocative: his universal world view, the missionary zeal with which he worked; undeterred by the personal cost involved, the openness of his art, and finally his preference for what were, on the whole, the simplest of materials. What provided the most important and profound impetus in his artistic approach was probably the idea of an *extended concept of art* - a concept which was a matter of pragmatism rather than philosophy, for it included not only traditional techniques and disciplines such as painting, sculpting and printing, but all creative activities in all spheres of human existence. His art was based on the idea that everything is in a state of flux, i.e. that a work of art cannot be pinned down to certain criteria, categories or forms. In principle, an advanced work of art must be understood as being open-ended, open also to the influenced of an empirical reality. Beuys's extended concept of art functioned as one of the most decisive factors in the discussion about the avant-garde, opening new perspectives for the future.

Just how emphatically Beuys's thoughts and actions were geared towards concrete reality can be seen in his preference for very simple and seemingly insignificant types of material. Like many other artists, Beuys gave new dignity and a new purpose to things which had been rejected, discarded and used up. His art became an unmistakable testimony against a society which cultivated the throwing-away of things. What is more, the potential open-endedness of his work flatly contradicts the self-contained world view of the world which is often portrayed by photography and the technological media. It also contradicts the ideas of a hedonistic society which believes that human problems can be solved by pressing a button – as if life were a T.V. soap opera.

It should not come as a surprise, therefore, that Beuys's art demands active participation on the part of the viewer, rather than passive enjoyment. Every part, every detail of his works must be examined very closely and given due attention, must be made to speak for itself, before we can gain any understanding of its broad spectrum. Very often details are no more than optical signals which trigger off both thought processes and intense emotional responses. Beuys's theory of art can best be summed up in his own words: "Thinking is sculpting."

And in fact this statement can only be fully understood if it is taken literally. The human brain is not an inert mass; it undergoes physiological changes whenever a person thinks. An artist can do no more than initiate thought processes. If he is successful, he has achieved his paramount aim. Physical changes in a person's brain indicate that thought processes are taking place, and if all the signs of a work of art are formulated accurately, they will show the way to more knowledge. Despite all the emotional reactions which his art has called forth, the real addressee was always the mind.

Andy Warhol's art was also based on an extended concept of art. His premises, however, were not universalist, and he lacked any utopian dimension. Unlike all other great Pop Artists, Warhol never sought to elevate the images of mass culture through aesthetic means.

Joseph Beuys:
The End of the 20th Century, 1983
Das Ende des 20. Jahrhunderts
Installation
Galerie Schmela, Düsseldorf

He simply left those screaming monuments of paper, cardboard and tin in all their banal brutality, and even enhanced their effect by duplicating or producing whole series of them. He made sculptures by simply arranging waste packaging material, which already anticipated the rigid aesthetic principles of Minimal Art. He erected pyramids of super-abundance with soup cans, and he elevated Marilyn Monroe, Hollywood's angel of sin, to the same level as Leonardo da Vinci's Mona Lisa. "Everything is beautiful" was his motto, and when he appeared in public he displayed – or seemed to display – a certain detached lack of concern, an aloofness with an appearance of zombie-like indifference, so that he came to be regarded as the typical, average man who merely shrugs his shoulders at all the daily disasters and catastrophes. While Beuys tried to warn people, Warhol simply recorded facts. According to the French theoretician of civilization Jean Baudrillad, the real disaster already consists in the fact that disasters can be brought about at all. Whereas Beuys would shake people up, Warhol realized that shaking them up with his art was merely another way of maintaining the gigantic entertainment machine. Hundreds of portraits of Marilyn Monroe destroy the apparent uniqueness of the painting which, originally a photographic representation, can never do more than simulate reality anyway. It is not until the image becomes independent and detached from the person to whom it owes its existence that it turns into an autonomous factor of our modern consumer society. The painting virtually absorbs the model, until it vanishes altogether. Although the circumstances of Marilyn's physical death were tragic, they confirmed the superiority of her photographic image, thus reducing her individual characteristics and claims to the size of charming idiosyncrasies or cranky whims.

Warhol was the first post-avant-garde artist. His art reflects the development of that second-hand reality which consists of mass-produced components created by the technological media, as well as the simple, repetitive formulas of the consumer world. Warhol, however, was far more aware of the consequences of this development for contemporary art than his

Joseph Beuys:
Fond VII/2, 1985
Interior installation
Galerie Schmela, Düsseldorf

colleagues, and indeed he became its conscious promoter. As a pragmatic American, though, he was still able to step back and look at his country through the amazed eyes of a foreigner, and he tried to influence the whole process instead of being crushed by it. When he launched his influential art magazine *Interview*, he created an instrument which acted as a mediator between serious art and mass culture, two spheres which had drifted apart. For a while he even managed a famous pop group called Velvet Underground. What was extraordinary was his feeling for the vitality of a cultural movement in which daring innovations mingled with trivial, standardized patterns, badly groomed forms of commercial art with the aesthetic demands of the avant-garde, and the tremolo of emotions with clearly intelligible appeals to reason. Warhol put himself at the top of this movement, thus lending practical substance to the concept of the avant-garde. It was a venturesome balancing act, which only succeeded because the artist, with his unfailing intuition for the artificiality of the world around him, managed to beat it at its own game. Even the ghastly attempt on his life by a radical feminist turned out to be a grand – though not deliberate – publicity stunt for him and his legendary *Factory*, the place where he produced both his artistic and his commercial products.

Unlike Beuys, Warhol did not regard the change of art into the 'art scene' as any great loss, nor did he mourn over the lost spontaneity and naturalness. Even after his death, it seems that – in retrospect – he was more contemporary than his German counterpart, because he simply accepted the artificiality of our world and – at best – drew people's attention to it by endlessly duplicating certain motifs. His portraits of Beuys show that he was an excellent observer of the art scene. In Warhol's gallery of celebrities Beuys can be seen side by side with the stars and super-stars of show business as well as politics, economics and history. Warhol's message: nobody can avoid being sucked into the whirlpool of the commercial mass media, unless he is happy not to have his ideas published. However, as soon as he becomes public, he necessarily has to play the game.

"The mysteries take place at the central railway station, not at the Goethe Grammar School."
Joseph Beuys, 1984

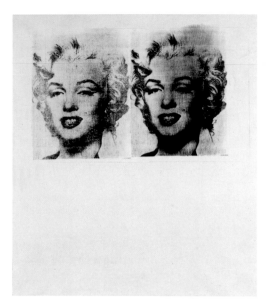

Andy Warhol:
Marilyn Twice, 1962
Acrylic and liquitex on canvas, screenprint,
29⅛ × 14⅛ in. (74 × 36 cm)
Marx Collection, Berlin

Andy Warhol:
Single Elvis, 1964
Screenprint on canvas, 82⅝ × 42⅛ in.
(210 × 107 cm)
Neue Galerie, Ludwig Collection, Aachen

Warhol knew the rules of the game perfectly. He was both the driving force and the object of the game, of the machine which promises fifteen minutes of fame. According to his friends, it was this idea of fame – or rather, publicity – which had propelled the artist from the very beginning. He played the game perfectly - the only game which met with the unconditional approval of Western society. And his methods were purer than those of any politician or film star – with no pretence of morality or self-pity. Does an artist have to be morally sound to be accepted as an artist? Such a question was utterly irrelevant to Warhol. His artistic world was not a world without morals, but a world beyond traditional morality, a world of doubles and clones who were constantly playing new roles, but whose first and foremost aim was that of being at the centre of public attention. "Andy has made paintings, drawings, sculptures and films. He has written a theatre play and a novel. He illustrated a cookery book and acted in films. He was the owner of a nightclub and the editor of a magazine. He directed commercials and acted in them himself. He became a photographer and a model. The only thing Andy has always tried but never achieved was perhaps that of becoming a rock star. He told me he had started a group together with Walter de Maria, Lucas Samaras and Patti Oldenburg, but after a few rehearsals they refused to let him go on singing. So he became the manager of Velvet Underground." (Glenn O'Brian)

Warhol continually quoted, used and re-shaped the glittering myths of the consumer world, which seize people but do not trouble them as the long-forgotten myths of the history of mankind do. The new myths have been given substance by photography, and it is in the glamorous superficiality of photography that they manifest themselves: as soon as a photo has been taken, it has already become part of the past. But although it is ephemeral, it continues to exist in the form of an illusory reflection – destined to be consumed quickly, while at the same time repeatable and therefore ready to be consumed again. Warhol enabled fashion to enter the realm of art, but in doing so he merely legitimized something that had already become an acceptable pattern. He was the most perfect protagonist of American culture, that fascinating structure in which reality and illusion intermingle, where the model and its copy have become interchangeable, because the photograph is "there" immediately, right next to the model, reducing to zero any distance in time so that the artificial image often seems like a double. The excessive abundance of visual stimuli, the overpowering presence of the here-and-now, the enormous wealth of consumer goods, the artificial rituals of people's social lives, the dissolution of uniqueness through fragmentation and repetition – this is how we can summarize the phenomena which add up to a certain cultural image, an image that was created by Warhol and is now generally associated with the name *America* .

And so it seems as if there were two almost opposing cultures - Germany (or rather, Europe) and America. The one appears to be dominated by dark forebodings, as if seeking refuge in the myths of the past because of a contradictory reality that has become bewildering and confusing, with a basic feeling of catastrophe and gloom, whereas one cannot avoid the impression that the other culture is virtually bursting at the seams with its shrill optimism and its obsession with the present. Can we say then that Beuys is the magician and Warhol the ingenious impresario of the age of technology? Clichés are certainly helpful when it comes to creating new trademarks, but they can be a hindrance if we want to do full justice to the subject matter at hand. There has been a tendency to neglect those elements in Beuys's art which are oriented towards the future, and also his rather positive understanding of technology, often reflected in his use of batteries as a metaphor. Conversely, Warhol's artificial world is based on elements which signal emptiness and isolation. The point where both artists meet is their attitude to mythology, although they both concentrate on different periods. Mythology is history in a condensed form, the pre-historic age of the nations before anything was recorded. The images of mythology express man's primaeval experiences which have sunk to the depths of the unconscious mind. The myths of our industrial civilization and modern welfare society express precisely those suppressed desires, secret anxieties, compensatory daydreams and yearnings for paradise on earth, and they do so in paintings and metaphorical images which bear witness to the power of the visual world – despite all literacy and culture.

Beuys and Warhol began a new chapter in the history of contemporary art. Not all their ideas have fallen on fertile ground, and only very few artists have fully understood their aesthetic philosophies. Following the demands of the sixties, they achieved the union of art and life, though the one tended more towards life, while the other had made a definite commitment to art, or rather to the artificiality of life. There can be no doubt that Beuys and Warhol acted as bridge-builders and avoided the dead end of Minimalist aesthetic principles – an achievement for which they will always be remembered.

Their deaths, however, also marked the end of an important chapter in contemporary art. While Beuys still created counter-images of day-to-day life with its seductive promises and continuous threats, Warhol went beyond this reality and neutralized it, so to speak, with his "super-paintings". In a sense, of course, Warhol's paintings are also counter-images, although the reality from which they are derived is that of second-hand paintings as produced by the mass media, i.e. paintings which reflect empirical reality by means of "art" and glamour.

Andy Warhol:
Twenty Jackies, 1964
Acrylic and liquitex on canvas, screenprint,
80½ × 80½ in. (204.5 × 204.5 cm)
Marx Collection, Berlin

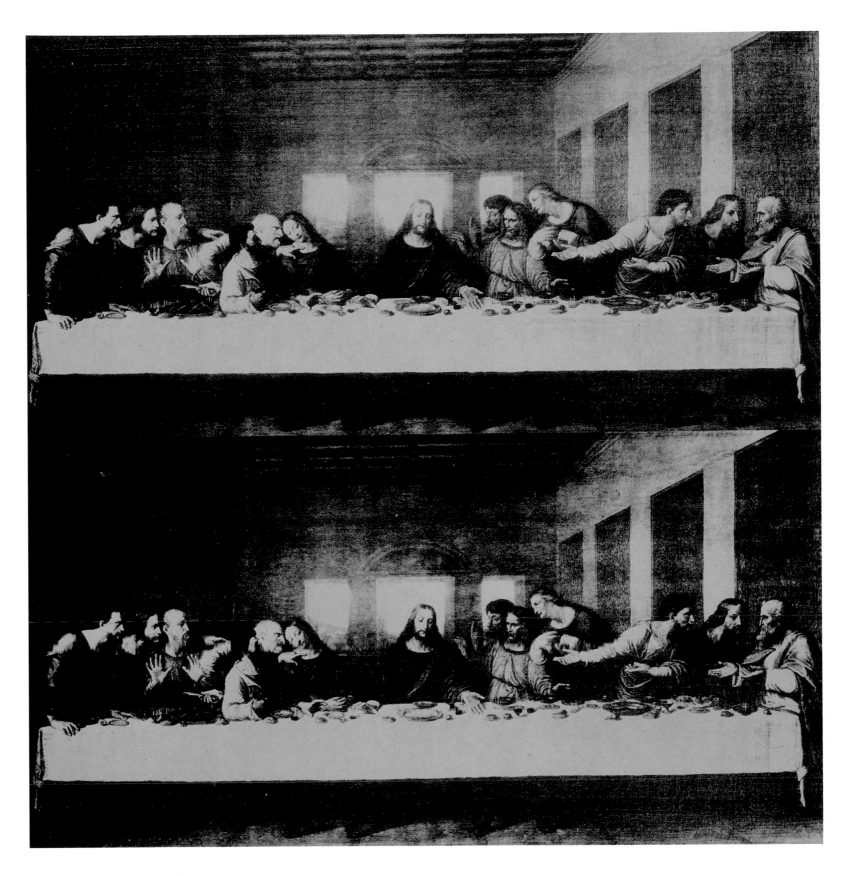

Andy Warhol:
Last Supper, 1986
Acrylic and liquitex on canvas, screenprint,
40 × 40 in. (101.5 × 101.5 cm)
Emily and Jerry Spiegel Collection,
New York

German Art – American Art

Once it had become clear that the world was not going to be saved by the German race, it was taboo for quite a long time to try and identify any Germanness in West German art or to trace its roots in cultural traditions. The new order of the day was internationalism, and it seemed that by suppressing their own cultural heritage German artists were trying to forget the style of the Nazi regime. They fervently copied ideas from France and the U.S., and occasionally also from Italy. Western art, particularly in its abstract forms, had become a synonym for the freedom which the Allied Forces had brought to Germany. Furthermore, the Cold War turned this art into a philosophical weapon. In view of the fact that such art forms were strictly prohibited in East Germany, the ideological pioneers of the Western version of abstract art seemed all the more persuasive. What was valued by the ruling political party in East Germany was above all the traditions of Realism – a school whose contemporary version was reviled as Socialist Realism in West Germany. Any artist who refused to bow to the doctrine of abstract art was in danger of being suspected of being a socialist or even a communist. Consequently, German artists were not particularly popular in other Western countries, because their endeavours, however authentic, were generally dismissed as inferior imitations. This is another way in which Beuys was totally innovative. Since his international breakthrough in the seventies, the term "German Art" has acquired a completely new meaning, and at times it has even had the sales-effective qualities of a "trademark". And yet, Beuys was an important pacemaker, although he always acknowledged his own past and that of his nation – a past which he regarded as his heritage – without denying or suppressing anything whatsoever. And he never left any doubt that, in his understanding of German heritage, Goethe, Hitler, the classicism of Weimar and the misguided spirit of Nazism were inextricably linked. His entire art is permeated by a sense of deep sadness at what had happened, a continuous call to mourn – something which only very few Germans are prepared to do.

Although Beuys was extremely important for Germany's entry into the international art scene, his art itself actually turned out to be so difficult and awkward that access to it did not become any easier even when it could be earmarked *German*. But as this label has now become genuinely sales-effective, there is a tendency to attach it to the paintings of other German artists who have also been defying the doctrines of abstract art. These are artists who picked up the supposedly lost thread of representational traditions, in particular the expressive ones. Baselitz is one of them, and so are Lüpertz, Penck, Jörg Immendorff and Kiefer. Their paintings are often used as evidence that German Expressionism is going through a second revival. Since many people rashly come to the stereotyped conclusion that the terms *German Art* and *Expressionism* are identical, these artists are seen as representative examples of *German Art*. It seems irrelevant that the only paintings which bear even a remote and superficial resemblance to German Expressionism are the early works of Baselitz, and Immendorff's *Café Deutschland* series. The other works, however, are considerably further removed from the Expressionism of the *Brücke* painters than from Beuys. The Swiss art critic Theo Kneubühler was therefore quite right when he countered rash attempts at establishing such links by saying: "It is obvious that the painting (of these artists – K.H.) does not speak of a world consisting of certain meanings, but as a world in itself, and thus of the world as it is."

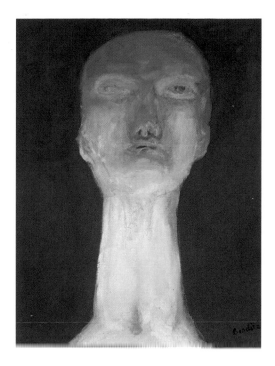

Georg Baselitz:
E.N. Idol, 1964
Oil on canvas, 39⅜ × 31½ in.
(100 × 80 cm)
Galerie Michael Werner, Cologne

Anselm Kiefer:
The Stairs, 1982/83
Die Treppe
Emulsion, oil and straw on canvas, photograph on document paper,
130 × 72⅞ in. (330 × 185 cm)
Private collection

Anselm Kiefer:
Ways of the World's Wisdom: the Battle of the
Teutoburg Forest, 1978
Wege der Weltweisheit: Die Herrmanns-
Schlacht
Wood engraving consisting of 31 parts, glued
together with Planatol BB Superior, blotting-
paper and hand-made paper, painted over with
acrylic and shellac, 126 × 141¾ in.
(320 × 360 cm)
Doris and Charles Saatchi, London

Kiefer's art, in particular, has been subjected to the most peculiar misinterpretations, many of which often reveal massive prejudices. This is all the more puzzling when one considers that Kiefer's art is not only stylistically removed from Expressionism, but also expresses a philosophy which is diametrically opposed to it. Unlike Emil Nolde, Karl Schmidt-Rottluff, Otto Mueller, Erich Heckel and Ernst Ludwig Kirchner, his landscapes do not conjure up the primaeval forces of nature, nor do they mystify them. The earth in his landscapes is burnt, it is an apocalyptic earth. His paintings are reminiscent of the image of nature in Romanticism and Expressionism, but in view of the acute threat to our world they also show how outmoded such images are. Even the straw which he sometimes uses in his paintings tells of times gone by. Images of green meadows, the rustling leaves of magnificent forests and rich fields only exist as memories. Kiefer's landscapes are filled with sorrow, rather than delight in ruin and destruction.

Likewise, the myths which the artist invokes have lost their mythical innocence because they have become history. Mythology does not have a present, a past or a future – unlike history. The myths depicted in Kiefer's paintings are the ones that have been perverted by German history. They were perverted in order to justify and disguise unimaginable crimes. These are the problems which are dealt with in Kiefer's paintings, not some petty obsession with the superiority of the German race.

Anselm Kiefer:
To the Unknown Painter, 1982
Dem unbekannten Maler
Oil, straw, wood-engraving on canvas,
110¼ × 134¼ in. (280 × 341 cm)
Boymans van Beuningen Museum, Rotterdam

There can be no doubt that one of Kiefer's most dominant themes is the history of his country. And so inevitably there are parallels with the art of Immendorff, Penck and – to a lesser extent – certain series of paintings by Baselitz and Lüpertz. Kiefer's main topic, however, is the immediate past, i.e. twelve years of state-organized Nazi terror. However, the artist is not a historian and does not pretend to be one. He does not see his work as an analysis, but rather as a diagnosis of the time. His understanding is as complex as Beuys's interpretation of reality, whose student he was for a while. His paintings are therefore not mere illustrations of historical events. They are mental images, or – more precisely – cognitive images. Many of them are soaked with bitter irony and open sarcasm, as in Kiefer's painting *Operation Sea Lion*, named after the code name of the operation during the Second World War in which the German navy was to conquer Britain. The attempt, which was given up before it was even started, is depicted ironically in the form of the German navy floating in a bath tub. And his series of large multi-media paintings on the Battle of the Teutoburg Forest (9 A.D.) – a magnificent combination of wood-cut, painting and collage – is not without an element of irony and sarcasm, either.

In these paintings Kiefer alludes to that mysterious battle fought by Herman the Cheruscan, or Arminius as he was called in Latin, by the enemies who had taught him the art of military warfare. In this battle he hit the supreme commander of the Roman Empire in Lower

Anselm Kiefer:
Painting the Burnt Earth, 1974
Malerei der verbrannten Erde
Oil on burlap, 37⅜ × 49¼ in.
(95 × 125 cm)
Private collection

Germany, Field Marshal Varus, on the head – a victory which has been regarded as a kind of ideological foundation stone of German history. In Kiefer's paintings, which are a conglomeration of men's heads stacked tightly in several rows and covered with lines like a spider's web, the Germanic chieftain is only one among many. His face is not even at the centre of the painting, but has been moved to one side, making room in one of these "historic panoramas" for the "cannon king", Alfred Krupp, whose head is enmeshed by the spider's web. It is a gallery of German heads in which there is contrast upon contrast. Writers and musicians can be seen side by side with military leaders and murderers such as Horst Wessel. It is obvious that Kiefer chose each name very carefully in this historical gallery of ancestors. Martin Heidegger and August Heinrich Hoffmann von Fallersleben, Stefan George and Heinrich von Kleist rub shoulders with Emperor William II of Prussia, the tough old Prussian veteran Albrecht Duke of Roon, Herman the Cheruscan and the arms manufacturer Krupp. Kiefer quite deliberately chose the ancient technique of wood-cuts, even though only for the background, with the collage emphasizing the tensions and the contradictions. However, Kiefer did not actually make authentic portraits of these historic figures but paraphrased well-known images of them which had become clichés in the minds of Germans. Thus Kiefer establishes a link between pictorial clichés and mental clichés. Are these characters dead and forgotten, buried under a spider's web, without any influence on people's consciousness, banished onto the pedestal of history? Or are they still alive, disturbing us by constantly upsetting our processes of suppression? Kiefer has re-discovered the art of historical painting,

Anselm Kiefer:
Sulamith, 1983
Emulsion, oil, acrylic, aquatex, shellac, straw
and wood- engraving on canvas, 116 × 148 in.
(290 × 370 cm)
Saatchi Collection, London

the royal genre of the 19th century. Nevertheless he approaches history with means that are fully appropriate, because they are equally historical. Using canvases that were once used for the celebration of victorious battles, with the thundering of cannons and the rolling of drums, Kiefer keeps awake the memory of death and destruction which is called to mind by merely mentioning the names of the battlefields. By trying to depict the horror, it is warded off and the terror taken out of it. This is why the most gruesome horror films at the cinemas serve as entertainment. Kiefer does not get caught in this trap.

Kiefer and Baselitz, Penck and Immendorff, Lüpertz and several others are above all painters, even though some of them turned to sculpture in the eighties. They even practised their craft when – under the pressure of Minimal Art and Concept Art – it was simply taken for granted that painting had become outmoded as a serious medium of artistic expression. However, there is one important point in which their art differs from any outmoded form of painting. They do not try to paint or copy nature, not even when – as does Baselitz and, frequently, Lüpertz – they make nature the object of their art. For, in a conventional sense, they do not depict or illustrate anything, nor do they create copies of anything. Rather, their paintings follow the avant-garde maxim that art is an independent artistic event that evokes mental associations, memories and thoughts which influence the flow of mental images in a human being. This is why their art is ambiguous, contradicting what appears to be the "truth" of the painted picture, which is only unambiguous with regard to the act of painting.

Baselitz's decision to paint his motifs upside-down has by now become a well-known

feature of his art. His aim is, first and foremost, to counteract conventional ways of looking at paintings and, following traditional patterns of perception, to prevent rash preconceptions. They are, above all, spheres of artistic action, and the tension inherent in each painting is also present in the subjects. This is due to the highly charged emotional atmosphere created by broad, at times even rough, brush-strokes. The art critic Kneubühler feels that Baselitz's paintings express a certain "aestheticism of stylistic breaches" which are intended to destroy the arbitrariness of our approach to art and the way in which we comment on it. This aesthetic concept can be seen very clearly in the way Baselitz turns motifs upside down. According to Kneubühler, it is usually only within a certain context that we look at a work of art and discuss it, so that there is a discrepancy between the intention of the painter and our interpretation of the painting. He points out, however, that this no longer applies to Baselitz's work: "The paintings are free from the context of certain thought patterns in which a painting is first and foremost a painting. It is not the product of a certain automatic procedure, but controlled by the structural network of the elements contained in the upside-down motifs. The painting is an autonomous, controlled, sensual object which is not related to anything but itself, so that it must be seen as part of the world and not as a text or comment on the world."

However, regardless of Baselitz's actual intentions, his work did promote a return to representational painting. And the more it gained ground, the more it shook the very foundations of abstract art – tenets which until then practically no one would have dared to challenge. When the artist's paintings began to gain access to museums in the second half of the seventies, it was not just a coincidence that he turned to sculpting. His sculptures, however, are more clearly inspired by Expressionism than his paintings, and there is a certain primaeval impact about these roughly hewn wooden sculptures with their emphatic colours. They marked the beginning of a new phase in Baselitz's work, caused – as before – by a radical break. They are sculptures by a painter, and as such closely related to his paintings. Other painters soon followed his example and began to sculpt or at least worked in both mediums. Penck, Immendorff, Lüpertz and Karl Horst Hödicke are all painters who had decided in favour of representational art with Expressionist tendencies.

One of the most interesting artists among them is Immendorff. As one of Beuys's students, he took an active interest in his teacher's art as well as his personality. Immendorff's artistic career has been rather a turbulent one. He started off as a painter with a strong political commitment, someone with great confidence in the working classes, who would use his art to protest vigorously against America's Vietnam War. He then made a surprising U-turn, and in his impressive series of pictures called *Café Deutschland* as well as in several other projects he concerned himself with the division of Germany into two separate states. He had been inspired by Renato Guttuso's masterpiece *Café Greco* and influenced by Penck, a close friend of his who was still living in East Germany at the time. One particularly decisive factor in his artistic career was the exhibition *Das tun, was zu tun ist* (Do What Has to Be Done), organized by the Westfälischer Kunstverein (Westphalian Art Society) in Münster in 1973. The exhibition catalogue was an unremitting statement of the lives of artists under the avant-garde banner, a radical rejection of a self-sufficient, politically neutral art, and a prime example of politically committed art. The motto was: "An artist's fist is also a fist." This does not mean that Immendorff was ham-fisted as a painter, but his art was overtly political and aimed at causing a stir. However, neither the exhibition nor the catalogue were seen by the desired audience. The artists who were being challenged did not start to serve the cause of propagandist art. Nor did the average, working-class Joe Bloggs feel particularly inclined to go to the exhibition. In one of the pictures – a double painting – the hope was expressed that on May 1st, 1973, Joe Bloggs would join a procession together with his mates and, waving the red flag, insist on his rights, rather than doing what he had done the year before – go for a picnic and simply have fun. But even if the exhibition had failed to achieve its social and political objectives, it certainly had an unmistakable effect – not only for Immendorff the artist – though this effect was obscured by the obvious political edge of the paintings. Its greatest repercussions could be felt in the sphere of art and aesthetics. For, in the early seventies, the Westfälischer Kunstverein in Münster was a stronghold of the avant-garde and, along with the museums in Krefeld and Mönchengladbach, one of the most important forums for that brittle and hermetically closed movement called Concept Art, i.e. the artistic direction which was compatible with the avant-garde theory that a work of art should be

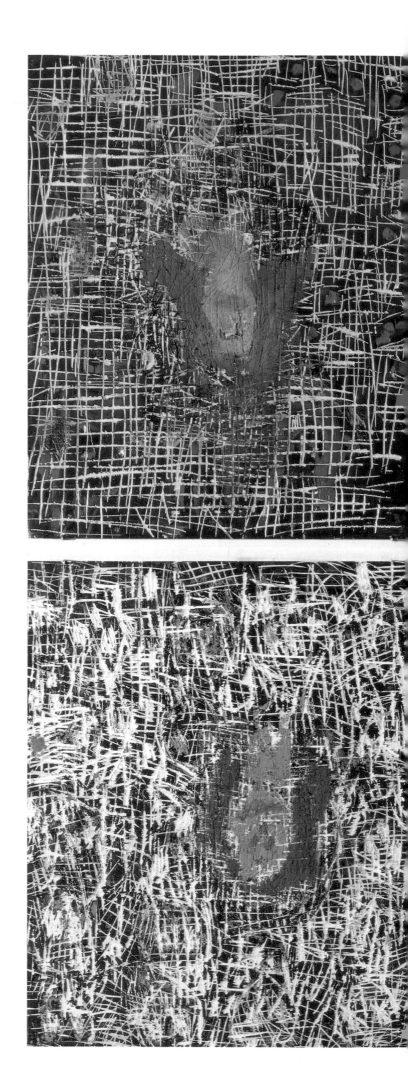

Georg Baselitz:
„45", 1989
Installation photograph: Georg Baselitz
Oil, tempera, carvings, wood,
20 pieces, each 78 ⅝ × 63 ⅝ in.
(200 × 162 cm)
Galerie Michael Werner, Cologne

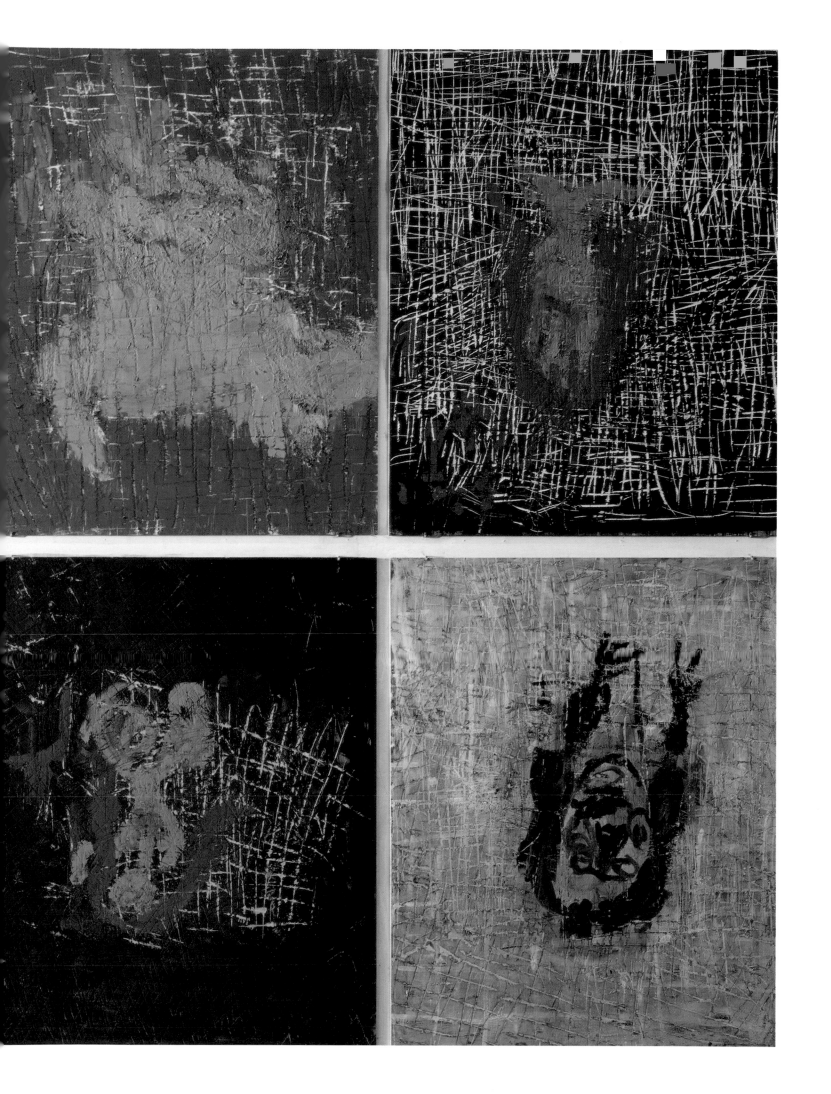

autonomous. It was hardly surprising, therefore, that a public which tended towards abstraction and spirituality was extremely irritated by Immendorff's poster-like and glowingly colourful paintings. Nevertheless, the scandal which had been expected by the artist and many of his like-minded friends did not take place. This exhibition, which was Immendorff's first one-man show in a museum, heralded the paradigmatic change which was to determine the art of the eighties. It was only just under a year since Baselitz had had his first museum exhibitions in West Germany.

However, the first impetus for a dramatic change in contemporary art was caused by a movement which was so specifically American in character that Europeans looked upon it as rather insignificant. Indeed, if it was given any attention at all, it was regarded with a good deal of bias and contempt. Externally, its main features are an overwhelming wealth of bright, even garish colours, a carefree delight in decorative effects and a preference for the ornamental, which had been scorned for quite a while, daringly merging representational and abstract elements while at the same time provocatively going back to folklore and cloth patterns. All in all, in view of the purist vocabulary of Minimal Art and Analytic Painting, these features were bound to be regarded as extremely dubious and outrageous. It was an artistic trend which was first called Pattern Painting and later became famous under the name Pattern & Decoration (P & D).

These labels – which, incidentally, were chosen by the artists themselves – may sound rather derogatory to Northern European ears, and yet accurately express the goals and intentions, as well as the most salient characteristics, of these artistic endeavours. Kushner, one of the most prominent representatives of P & D, explained which qualities a work of art with this label should have: firstly, it should be two-dimensional rather than trying to create an illusion; secondly, it should be expansive rather than introverted; thirdly, patterns - including pre-fabricated ones – should be incorporated; and fourthly, the subject or meaning

Jörg Immendorff:
Pot, 1985
Topf
Oil on canvas, 112¼ × 98½ in.
(285 × 250 cm)
Galerie Michael Werner, Cologne

Markus Lüpertz:
Ghosts in the Spaces: Eurystheus II, 1987
Zwischenraumgespenster: Eurystheus II
Oil on canvas, 63 × 78¾ in.
(160 × 200 cm)
Galerie Michael Werner, Cologne

Page 65:

Markus Lüpertz:
Melon Mathematics XVIII, 1984/85
Melonenmathematik XVIII
Oil on canvas, 47 × 38⅛ in.
(122 × 97 cm)
Galerie Michael Werner, Cologne

A.R. Penck:
Looking Back at the Quiet Bay, 1977
Blick rückwärts in die stille Bucht
Dispersion on canvas, 56⅝ × 70½ in.
(144 × 179 cm)
Galerie Michael Werner, Cologne

A.R. Penck:
N – Complex, 1976
N – Komplex
Dispersion on canvas, 112¼ × 112¼ in.
(285 × 285 cm)
Galerie Michael Werner, Cologne

Robert Kushner:
Sail Away, 1983
Mixed media and acrylics, 87 × 206 in.
(221 × 523.2 cm)
Holly Solomon Gallery, New York

Jörg Immendorff:
Ambassador on Grass, 1967
Botschafter über Gras
Dispersion on canvas, 7⅞ × 9⅞ in.
(20 × 25 cm)
Neue Galerie, State Art Collection, Kassel

of the painting should be secondary to its visual effect. In other words, a work of art should not be concerned with transcendence, but wholly and completely with the here and now. Reality should be applied, not penetrated. It should aim to change people's tastes, not their awareness, replacing Puritan barrenness with baroque opulence.

Pattern & Decoration combines stimuli from a vast range of traditions, especially from non-European cultures, which explains why it has met with so little appreciation in Europe. In particular, it has been influenced by the bright colours of Iranian Islamic art with its complex repertoire of engravings, the landscapes and erotic motifs of the Far East, Mexican tiles, Moorish architecture, Moroccan ceramics and early American quilts. Other influences include Robert Rauschenberg's *Combine Paintings*, Pop Art with its taste for the banal, and the whole wealth of industrially manufactured printed patterns and wallpaper. The materials which are used by artists like Kushner, MacConnel, Shapiro, Thomas Lanigan-Schmidt and Joyce Kozloff are usually no more than loosely draped pieces of cloth. These are taken from the "upper" as well as the "lower shelves" or echelons of cultural history, thus amalgamating and forming fascinating ensembles without any claim to universal validity, and combining social criticism (as in MacConnel's and Shapiro's art) with a certain *joie de vivre*.

Such artistic tendencies, which constitute "a movement rather than a style" (Robert Jensen and Patricia Conway), were bound to seem like a head-on attack on the sacred principles of avant-garde art. Two aspects particularly emphasized the radical difference between P & D and the avant-garde. On the one hand, there was the refusal to subscribe to the concept of an autonomous work of art that sets its own boundaries and develops its own reality, not owing anything to anybody. Instead, P & D artists preferred to see a work of art as a vessel which contained a wide range of different influences, with a general openness towards tradition as well as present-day reality, its aim being to impress, overwhelm and fascinate, with an explicit commitment to the functional character of art. On the other hand – and this is a closely related aspect – it consciously sought to display an approach that is historical, eclectic and pluralistic. In this respect Pattern & Decoration already manifested a fair number of attitudes that were typical of the post-avant-garde. And when Becker, the museum curator mentioned above, attempted to compare the obsessive works of some of these artists with the paintings of Baselitz, Lüpertz, Penck and Kiefer – even though he only did this once – it probably told us more about German art than it may have seemed.

One of the most important results, both socially and politically, of Pattern & Decoration has been the enormous boost in prestige for female artists. It was an artistic movement that secured women a legitimate place in contemporary art, whereas until then they had been no more than marginally respected outsiders. Certain techniques in women's art, such as weaving, sewing and the imaginative variation and repetition of pre-arranged shapes and patterns, have always been regarded as typically female spheres and have therefore never

Page 69:

Kenny Scharf:
Jungle Jism, 1985
Oil, acrylic and enamel spraypaint on canvas,
112 × 81½ in. (284.5 × 207 cm)
Neue Galerie, Ludwig Collection, Aachen

Kim MacConnel:
Paintings and Occasional Chairs
Installation view, Holly Solomon Gallery,
New York, 27th April – 19th May 1984

been regarded as particularly prestigious or valuable cultural activities. Shapiro was therefore fully justified in regarding P & D as an explicitly political art form, an artistic means of expression which promoted the emancipation of women, at least in the field of art.

Furthermore, P & D made an important contribution to breaking down barriers between art and architecture, a wall which had become insuperably high under the banner of the avant-garde. No wonder, therefore, that Kushner interprets his own art and that of his friends as an artistic reaction to the barrenness of modern shoebox architecture. It was the same barrenness, he said in an interview with Robin White, that could be observed in the designs of textile patterns and furniture as well as avant-garde art, which – incidentally – he called "classical" art. By contrast, Pattern & Decoration does not make a basic distinction between art and commercially manufactured patterns, with the one exception that a painting must always be composed as a whole, whereas material which is sold by the metre depends very much on the repetition of a continuous programme. Kushner also feels strongly that there is a definite place for a decorative element in art. This, he says, need not necessarily be pretty or flattering, but it can just as easily be aggressive. Anyone who believes that Pattern & Decoration is no more than one of those numerous passing stylistic fancies which rapidly succeeded one another after the Second World War does not realize how highly explosive this new aesthetic approach is, and therefore fails to do justice to artists like Kushner, MacConnel, Shapiro and Ned Smyth. Their art poses questions that go to the very core of contemporary art. And, likewise, since *Art Nouveau, Art Deco, Bauhaus* and *De Stijl* there has not been such a massive challenge to contemporary architecture as with Pattern & Decoration. Many of the artists have by now put their ideas into practice in the form of public or private internal and external arrangements, thus proving the immense durability of their artistic ideas. With Pattern & Decoration, contemporary art has re-conquered a social dimension which was largely negated by the avant-garde for conceptual reasons.

Thomas Lanigan-Schmidt:
The Preying Hands, 1983
Installation, 155⅛ × 356⅝ in.
(394 × 884 cm)
Holly Solomon Gallery, New York

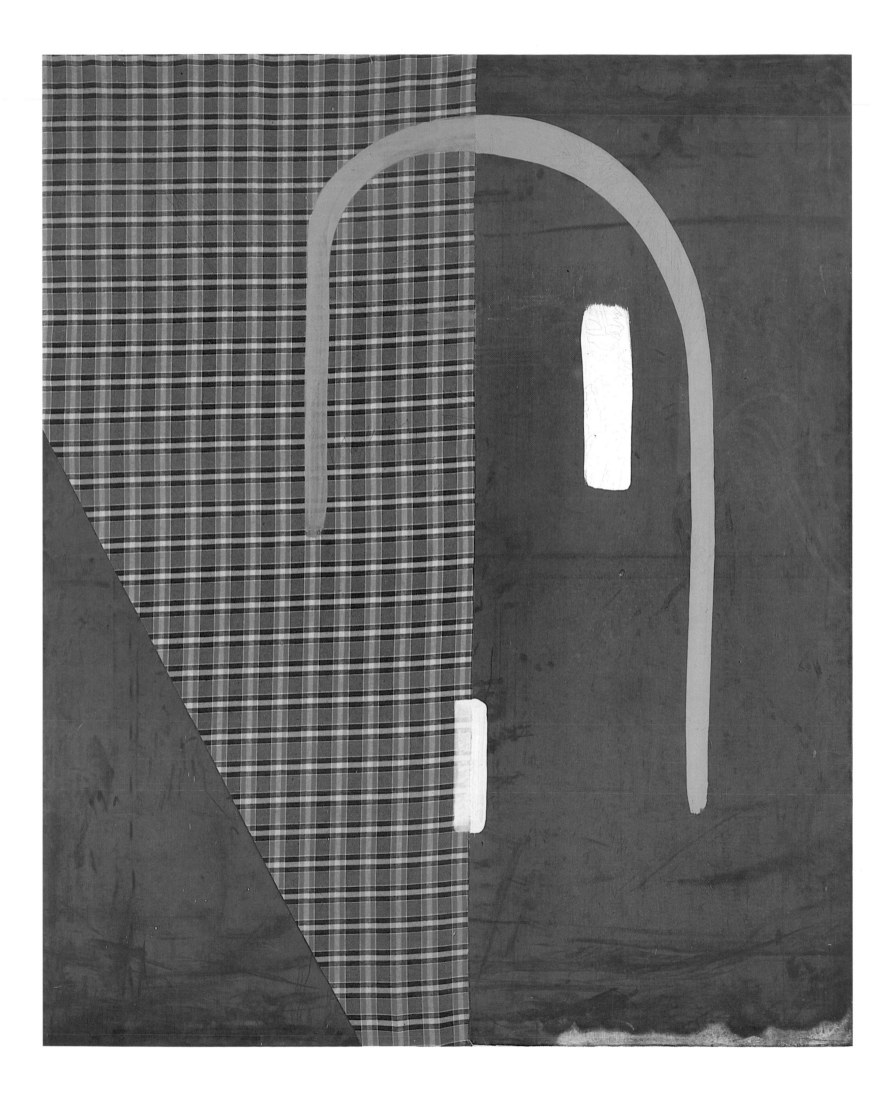

Pictures in a World of Pictures

Wherever you look, there are pictures – photographic pictures in newspapers and magazines, on advertising posters, both large and small, suggestive cinematic pictures, pictures which – in the light of the projectors – acquire a reality of their own, and of course the omnipresent pictures of television. German sitting-rooms are illuminated by televised pictures for an average of four hours every day, and American sitting-rooms nearly all day long. Not to mention the innumerable private photographs, movie films and video films of people's latest holidays or family get-togethers. The pictures of art are faced with tough competition. No society has ever been more obsessed with pictures than that of the Western hemisphere in the 20th century. Photography has succeeded in mechanizing the scientific image of the Renaissance, which subjected all data of the visible world to the visible reality of a central vanishing point. Mass distribution gives credibility to exact copies of reality. Film and T.V. have probably changed the effect of a picture and increased it in a way nobody would have anticipated, but the images projected onto the screen still obey the same rules. Truthfulness is ascribed to these mechanical and electronic pictures, and they can be used as evidence in court, though of course it is only photographs that are considered incapable of lying. The extent to which such a photographic view of the world has influenced our vision and thoughts can be seen quite easily in the specific development of contemporary art. On the one hand, there are those pictures which defy any attempt to interpret them as reproductions of real life. They do not depict anything at all, but have to be perceived and understood in their own right, as autonomous pictures. On the other hand, there are those pictures which have been inspired by photography without, however, being photographic copies or duplicates.

Gerhard Richter, who is one of the most important German painters in the international art scene, painted from photographic images for quite a long time. However, unlike American Pop Artists, he used to take very little interest in the industrially manufactured products of the mass media. Indeed, it was only very rarely that he took illustrations from newspapers and magazines, and he did so only when they expressed an element of grief and sorrow. He was far more interested in the amateur photographs that one finds in family albums. It was not from spectacular photographs that he derived his subjects. He had no time for photos which glorified the earthly paradise of the consumer world, nor did he take any interest in photography of a more artistic kind. Instead he drew on the trivial spheres of culture, such as illustrations in the daily press, ordinary, everyday private photos, which people had taken for their own enjoyment. At first he used holiday snaps, and when his artistic concept became more sophisticated, photographs from every sphere of life. What these photos have always had in common is that they are all taken from a perspective which is almost totally uniform and therefore appears to be objective – an extremely widespread point of view. With these photographs, Richter established a distance between his paintings and the real world, while at the same time endowing the actual subjects with an element of objectivity. He understood photographic reality as a reality in its own right, an independent world. And so his paintings were never about the world depicted in the original photographs, but rather about the photographic images as part of objective reality. Empirical reality is therefore reflected in a twofold manner in Richter's art, i.e. mechanically and manually, as a photograph and as a painting.

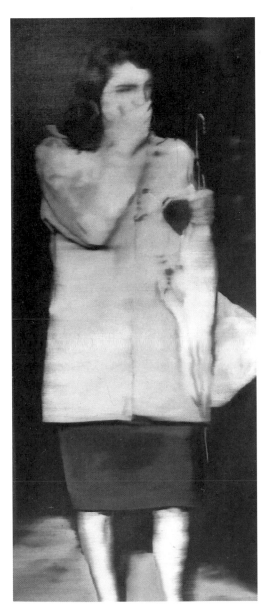

Gerhard Richter:
Woman with Umbrella (29), 1964
Oil on canvas, 63 × 37⅜ in.

Sigmar Polke:
Arch, 1965
Dispersion on decorative material,
78¾ × 64½ in. (200 × 164 cm)
Private collection

Using a painting by Titian called *Proclamation*, which marked a complete change of direction in the painter's art, Richter painted a variation on this theme which exemplified the entire intellectual gamut of his artistic programme. Just as photography has a certain technique of projecting all the phenomena of the visible world in the form of a special system of images, it also projects works of art in a special way. The photographic reproduction process manipulates the reproduced work of art and considerably affects its intentions. A photograph of a painting can never be more than a photograph of a painting. It is a photographic reproduction, not a painting. Richter was quick to realize this paradox and made it the basis for his aesthetic approach. Many of his paintings can be reduced to the motif of a photographic picture, and can be traced back to an original photograph, though they do not really lend themselves to any photographic rendering again. This gives them a certain self-sufficiency. Consequently the very reason which gets them people's attention becomes elusive, i.e. that aesthetic dimension which is the result of nothing but artistic practice. It follows that there is no real difference between Richter's "photographic" and "abstract" paintings (his colour tables consisting of hues from a paint catalogue and arranged in rectangular patterns) and his impenetrable "grey" paintings. It is only as originals that they unfold their full artistic quality, and the abstract element in Richter's art is not that of anti-pictures, but of autonomous artistic reality.

The photograph which Gerhard Richter used for his *Proclamation, after Titian* turned out to be an opportune trap. As a photographic reproduction it was part of the range of motifs familiar to the artist. However, as the photographic reproduction of a painting, with a subject matter that cannot be grasped intellectually, but which goes beyond the empirical world, reaching into a metaphysical realm, this image still contained elements of the transcendental. Richter's new "abstract" paintings, visual events and fictitious models for a reality which "eludes" the direct grasp of "theory and description" (Roald Nasgaard) have solved the problem of picture vs. reproduction, with artistic principles that prevailed before the avant-garde. His paintings must be understood as independent structures of reality, but also as reproductions of spheres of existence and experience that cannot yet be imagined. However, they differ from the tradition of painting as we know it in that they cannot be properly described. They show us a world which nobody has ever seen, a world beyond everyday experience. Although Richter does not disregard the demand that contemporary art should be autonomous, he nevertheless lays claim to functions in his own art that go far beyond this. "Being used to perceiving something real in a painting, we rightfully refuse to think of paint (in all its manifold aspects) as the only element that gives substance to a work of art. Instead we are content to look at something that has no substance at all, which has never been seen before and which is not visible. This is not a clever game but a necessity. Because the unknown generally frightens us, while at the same time giving us hope, we accept these paintings as a way of making the inexplicable a little more explicable, or at least more comprehensible."

Richter has been well-known and appreciated in West Germany since the late sixties, and his first solo exhibition outside an art gallery took place at the *Zentrum für aktuelle Kunst* (Centre for Topical Art) in Aachen in 1969. By contrast, however, it was quite some time before he was also recognized on a more international level. In the U.S., in particular, his art met with blank incomprehension. His continuous change of artistic methods, sometimes accompanied by a rapid change in motifs and occasionally with the same range, his emphatic insistence on the difference between the subject of a painting and its meaning, a topic and its depiction, was bound to produce a climate of uncertainty for as long as the public was used to consistency in the change of directions and styles.

Sigmar Polke was treated in a similar way. At times American art critics even believed that there was a close link between his art and Pattern & Decoration – for no other reason but that Polke, who enjoyed experimenting, occasionally used pieces of printed manufactured cloth in his paintings. It is not without justification that Richter and Polke are frequently mentioned in one breath. For several years they did indeed pursue similar goals, launched a number of artistic projects together, and even their aesthetic creeds are not entirely incompatible. In Polke's superbly painted pictures, his photographs and motion pictures, as well as in his few sculptures and spatial arrangements there is a formal mixture of different visual worlds. It is a combination of the artistic and the trivial, the manual and the industrially manufactured, the unbroken, artistic capital of the Dada movement, a breath of surrealistic speculation, a

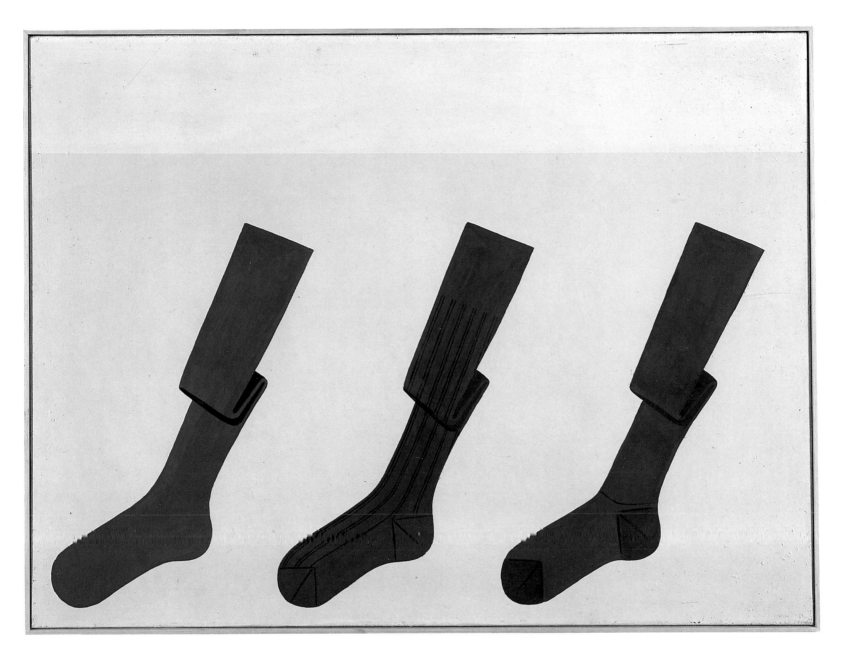

Sigmar Polke:
Socks, 1963
Socken
Varnish on canvas, 27½ × 39⅜ in.
(70 × 100 cm)
C.A.W. Collection

Sigmar Polke:
The Computer Moves In, 1983
Mixed media with manganese on decorative
material, 94½ × 126 in.
(240 × 320 cm)
Galerie Erhard Klein, Bonn

Sigmar Polke:
Camp, 1982
Lager
Dispersion and scattered pigment on decora
tive material and woollen blanket,
177⅛ × 98½ in. (450 × 250 cm)
Private collection

burning curiosity and an eager willingness to experiment and take risks. Although Polke's
artistic ideas have a different perspective and are expressed differently, he shares the
universality of Beuys: "Polke is universal: revolutionary, sensitive and merciless, a man with
vision and very human. He paints for museums and galleries, while at the same time despising
them. He paints religious scenes and black magic nightmares with the same expressiveness.
His obstinacy and passionate feelings are utterly untypical of a German and – like all great
geniuses – he combines universal experiences, such as the elegance of English portrait
painters, the glowing colours and gracefulness of Venetian genre-paintings, the intensity and
popular appeal of the Flemish, the mysterious and unexpected play of light and darkness in
Eastern prints." (Harald Szeemann)

Like Beuys, Polke's day-to-day attitudes are an inextricable part of his general artistic
strategy. His definition of art, though equally serious, contains a more playful element than
Beuys's, although it also includes the whole spectrum of reality. On the other hand, Polke's
attitude towards the world is shot through with irony so that his aesthetic concept is certainly
very different from Beuys's. Irony is a term which is frequently misunderstood, and an
ironical person is often seen as somebody who has withdrawn from everything because he
refuses to take anything seriously – a witty but irresponsible buffoon. In reality, however, he
is simply someone who reacts to the insipid emptiness of this non-committal world by
gradually removing himself from reality, and – as the literary critic Uwe Japp puts it –
plunging into "the sea of irony, though without the secure hope that there will be a firm land
of identity on the other side of the sea". It follows that Polke's daredevil balancing acts, his
supposed lack of seriousness, which seems to pervade his paintings of the sixties and
seventies, are no more than symptoms of the pain he feels at having removed himself from
reality. Being ironical, Polke perceives the world around him as unreal, grotesque, incongru-
ous, full of lies and deception, profoundly contradictory and devoid of any awareness of its
own contradictions. With his irony, however, even Polke is inextricably involved in this
world, with an odd kind of complicity. What makes his position so relevant is the fact that he is
continually trying to come to terms with this world, rather than denying it or seeking refuge in
the soothing haven of a dream world.

In ancient mythology irony was associated with the prophetically gifted god of the sea
Proteus, who was miraculously able to assume any shape he liked. "What is so protean about
him is the fact that he is always somebody else, and – paradoxically – this is how we are to
recognize him. The metamorphic nature of Proteus is undoubtedly part of the element to
which he belongs. And so another aspect reveals itself which retrospectively relates Proteus
to irony (and explains his name): not only does it show the complexity of irony, but it also
points to the element with which irony is frequently linked – the *sea of irony* in which an
ironical person is either at home, like a Leviathan, or shipwrecked." (Japp). And there are
indeed some obvious parallels between Polke's art and this description of Proteus. His art has
already been ascribed to numerous different movements. In his early paintings the world is
reflected and projected in a confusing variety and in several layers, so that the reality of the
original pictures add up to a distorted image of empirical reality – confusing, glaring, turning
things inside out and back to front, tightly packed, as if everything was going to collapse at the
same time. Our day-to-day experiences are distorted beyond recognition, but in such a way
that we can now understand them more clearly. His paintings of the eighties confront the
viewer with a cosmos of colours that have never been seen before, iridescent and dangerous
like the oil slicks on the oceans. Under the influence of light and atmosphere they sometimes
change completely and occasionally even disintegrate. The effect of his paintings – most of
which are quite large – is so overwhelming that one must plunge into them and lose oneself.

Looking at a painting becomes a daring adventure – an adventure that started when the
artist began to paint it and continues with the act of viewing it. It is an art of perpetual change.
Nothing is fixed, everything is fluid and interlinked, with only very few fixed lines or contours
that might lend support. One enters a visual world with no familiar landmarks. It is a reality
that reveals itself through seeing and feeling. Like a dream, it is fluid and intangible, with
nothing but apparitions, though without any conjuring tricks. It is a world in which there is no
longer any dividing line between good and evil, between beauty and horror. Many critics have
described Polke as a modern alchemist, and his studio as a magician's laboratory. It is
certainly true to say that the artist is prepared to take any risk whatever, even if it places him in
personal danger, in order to realize his visions artistically and to sensitize his addressee's

Sigmar Polke:
Alice in Wonderland, 1983
Alice im Wunderland
Mixed media on decorative material,
126 × 102⅜ in. (320 × 260 cm)
Galerie Erhard Klein, Bonn

Gerhard Richter:
Untitled (551-4), 1984
Oil on canvas, 17 × 23⅝ in. (43 × 60 cm)

warped power of perception. In the final analysis these paintings give the beholder a view of his inner soul; he is confronted with himself, as it were. "Polke's art has stimulated a new start in a discussion which has temporarily run aground and become one-sided, i.e. the discussion about 'what we mean when we talk about art'. This is because he took up this uncertainty and made it the very topic of his own work, using formulas and materials which combine the incompatible, i.e. the beautiful and the ugly, the rough and the smooth, abundance and scarcity, the delicate and the coarse, the trivial and the transparent. Day-to-day experiences are full of art, and art is full of everyday moments – in both spheres it is magic which waters the barren ground." (Stemmler)

Polke feels at home in all visual media. He is a visual maniac. There is not a single visual medium which he has left untouched and whose capacity to trigger off new experiences he has not explored. He always carries a camera with him, either for photographs or films. He constantly takes photos, and yet his photographic work is virtually unknown. The criteria which he applies to photographs are the same as for paintings, and when he paints he sometimes uses the chemical methods of photography. Polke is a genuine key figure in contemporary art. His art and his artistic standpoint, which are also apparent in his outward behaviour, have typecast him into this role, so that there are times when he can hardly escape from his followers. His confident use of all the possibilities and opportunities afforded by the visual arts, both popular and serious, manual and technological, his extraordinary ability to combine these options, his inexhaustible inventiveness as well as the ironical distance which he maintains, together with his undisguised subjectiveness – all these elements make Polke one of the foremost initiators of post-avant-garde art in the eighties. His studio at a farm in

Willich in the lower Rhine area was literally a laboratory (Peter Schjedahl) where many of those things were concocted which were to change the artistic landscape in later years. From time to time he was joined by Achim Duchow, Walter Dahn, Julian Schnabel and David Salle, to name but a few.

It has been a common phenomenon that whatever art was contemporary at a given point in time intensified and aggravated the general social tendencies, the conflicts and contradictions, the sudden changes, the new trends, mechanisms and structures – in other words, everything that is often summed up as *zeitgeist*. Elements which are concealed by society are revealed in art. This does not mean, of course, that artists are latter-day prophets, even though they often behave as if they were. Rather, they are the most sensitive and nervous instruments of the *zeitgeist*. However, it is only in their social role as artists that they are also instruments of the process of life, so that at best they function as prototypes and within manoeuvering space allocated to them by society. This is a sphere where the artist can experiment, i.e. it is not a mere playground for the pursuit of extravagance and luxury. The idea that both the artist and his art could be totally autonomous has always been fictitious. And yet this manoeuvering space is not subject to continuous control by society. The social space for experimentation in which the artist moves is not a laboratory which has to show practical results. It is a romping ground for creative personalities whose social value consists of their ability to produce works that continually question our hardened habits of perception whenever they have got into a rut, our thought patterns when they have turned into blue-prints and our emotional reactions when they have become routine. The feeling that society is in the throes of a profound crisis tends to be rather vague at first, but the more it rises to the

Gerhard Richter:
Group of Trees (628-1), 1987
Baumgruppe (628-1)
Oil on canvas, 28⅜ × 40⅛ in.
(72 × 102 cm)

Gerhard Richter:
Venice – Stairs with Isa (586-3), 1985
Venedig – Treppe mit Isa (586-3)
Oil on canvas, 19⅝ × 27½ in.
(50 × 70 cm)

surface, the more relentless will be the opposition of the defenders of traditional social norms. At the same time, however, there is also an increasing willingness to try out alternatives. Thus, in the midst of the widespread feeling of crisis at the end of our century, it is hardly surprising that one sector of anthropology has proclaimed King Proteus as the "typical hero of our time" (Eike Gebhardt), and the type of person to whom the future is said to belong is no longer the "authoritarian" character with a strong ego, but rather an unstable, yet creative person. The former is incarcerated in the prison of his own rigid ego, which refuses to allow the revision of any judgement once it has been made, regardless of whether it originally came from others and has simply been taken over or whether it has always been his own. The unstable, creative person, on the other hand, is flexible, prepared to change his course and – if his flexibility goes hand in hand with creative imagination – is also able to make independent judgements and decisions. Modern sociologists have diagnosed that the age of the mature, inner-directed personality of the old school has passed and that it has become "non-functional". And so one might indeed ask if perhaps the attitudes of someone like Polke, as well as those of other typical European and American artists of the eighties, are not the very embodiment of that new "unstable" – and yet "creative" – type of person described by the sociologists. Are artists now providing the model which the rest of society will follow?

We are currently living in a phase of profound and far-reaching social and historical upheaval, a period in which art has ceased to pursue its utopian dream of any substantial human identity, the union of mind and body, and the idea that the relationship between man and the world could proceed harmoniously without the intervention of death. And this blatant absence of continuity in life comes to light particularly clearly in works of art. The eminent art historian Ernst Gombrich once suggested that art has always developed along the lines of model and correction, and if he is right, then the seismological oscillations of society are heralded by breaches – sometimes hardly perceptible – of predominant artistic patterns. These provide, as it were, the basic conditions. The breaches of outmoded artistic patterns usually take two different forms: either as violently aggressive deformations or as ironical

Gerhard Richter:
Proclamation, after Titian (343-1), 1973
Verkündigung nach Tizian
Oil on canvas, 50⅜ × 110¼ in.
(128 × 280 cm)

disguises. Both manifestations have a common root. They signify a gulf between man and reality.

Reality has lost its uniform character and has disintegrated into numerous intricate sections which, in turn, can be divided and duplicated. In these different realities man is confronted with himself as a stranger and an alien. Periods of antagonism between man and the world have been the rule, and those of unity the exception – which is why the history of art has known very few periods of classicism, but an enormous number of anti-classicist movements.

Gerhard Richter:
Untitled (570-4), 1984
Oil on canvas, 25⅝ × 31½ in.
(65 × 80 cm)

Irony – Travesty – Clownish Antics

When we compare the elegant cubes of Minimal Art, the purist manifestations of Concept Art and the austere buildings of functional architecture with the paintings, sculptures, churches and mansions of the Italian High Renaissance, it may seem preposterous to describe today's art as "classical art". But is this really so outrageous? Nobody would deny that the historical period of Classicism had a glamourous sensuality verging on insolence, whereas the contemporary period (which has not yet become history) displays a certain sensual barrenness. But it was modern art which fulfilled something that had been heralded and only dreamed of in historical Classicism: an art of perfect dimensions and proportions – an intellectualized art. Is there only a superficial resemblance between New York, the pulsating capital of modern finance, and Florence, the ancient banking and trading centre in Northern Italy? During the Renaissance, which lasted for only a short time, art claimed to have reached a degree of almost divine perfection, and it was against this perfection that the creative spirit of the artists rebelled, in the form of what was then known as Mannerism. The late Raphael, the late Michelangelo – who, together with Leonardo, were the most outstanding protagonists of Renaissance art – even initiated this rebellion. Mannerism involved excessively refined poses, superb painting techniques, and witty allusions – but it was also an art of exuberant eroticism, formal discrepancies and disproportions, mute despair and secret horrors.

At a relatively early stage the Italian art critic Bonito Oliva pointed out the remarkable affinity between Mannerism and the art of the eighties. From his point of view this is quite understandable, because the link is quite obvious when we look at the paintings and sculptures of artists such as Sandro Chia, Francesco Clemente, Enzo Cucchi and Mimmo Paladino, whom he actively supported. Consider the bulging bodies of Chia's plump figures, or Clemente's complicated metaphors – so full of innuendo and visual surprise effects – or the mysterious bodiless faces and faceless bodies in Cucchi's art, or the multi-faceted narrative style of Paladino – a style that is reminiscent of classical murals and tapestries and shows familiarity with mosaics too. In all these paintings the world as we know it has been distorted. These artists emphasize what is charming, odd, risqué, they mobilize the myths of the past, unite the incompatible – Pablo Picasso and Marc Chagall, the art of Antiquity and of African tribes, dream and reality – and they operate within a whole range of glowing colours, sometimes verging on bad taste. Outwardly, of course, the special character of Mannerist paintings is totally different. Today's works of art do not have anything precious about them, nor are they particularly spiritual or programmatic. They are less desperate and more playful and rambling. Nevertheless, there are some striking parallels: the artist's assertion of his ego, his emphasis on extreme subjectivity, the physiological element, an obsession with the human body, including the occasional depiction of excrement which the *Mülheimer Freiheit* artists found so fascinating, the lack of homogeneity of the world they paint, the multiple fragmentation of the painting's structure, their tendency to narrate, and the unusual choice of colours. The similarities can be found chiefly in artistic attitudes, whereas in the works themselves they are mainly of a structural nature. Furthermore, today's Italian painters share a certain degree of restlessness with their Mannerist forerunners.

Although the Italian painters come from different parts of the country, there are relatively few regional elements in their paintings and sculptures. Longobardi is one of the few

"It is not enough to give signals. Things can only ever last if they have functioned as signs."
Enzo Cucchi, 1986

Sandro Chia:
Smoker with Yellow Glove, 1980
Fumatore con Guanto Giallo)
Oil on canvas, 57⅞ × 81⅞ in.
(147 × 208 cm)
Sammlung Bruno Bischofberger, Zurich
Küsnacht

From left to right:
Sandro Chia, Nino Longobardi, Mimmo
Paladino, Paul Maenz, Francesco Clemente
and his wife, Wolfgang Max Faust, uniden-
tified, Fantomas, Gerd de Vries, Lucio Amelio

Sandro Chia:
Hand Game, 1981
Oil on canvas, 72⅝ × 57⅞ in.
(184.5 × 147 cm)
Sammlung Bruno Bischofberger, Zurich
Küsnacht

exceptions, with paintings that breathe the spirit of his native Naples. But what is there in Clemente's works that is typical of Southern Italy? Or what might possibly be characteristic of Northern Italy in Chia's or Cucchi's art? Among these artists, Clemente is the one who has travelled most, and he is equally at home in East and West, in Europe, America and Asia. Cucchi is the most prolific, and in 1987 he had no less than four large solo exhibitions in West German museums. In his paintings Chia unites Picasso's Neo-Classicism with the dream like, poetic quality of Chagall, whereas in his sculptures he tends to emulate Auguste Rodin's monumentalism. In his tapestries Paladino interweaves the various mediaeval Christian cosmologies with the primitive cultures of Africa and South East Asia. Travelling, in the widest possible sense, has always been a recurring theme in the work of these artists, even though they may differ widely with regard to individual style and artistic world view, and this restlessness is also reflected in their continuously changing techniques.

In fact, it may have been this theme of self-discovery which made the paintings of these Italian artists landmarks of contemporary art at the beginning of the eighties – self-discovery in a world that is being shaken by one crisis after another, with an enormous gulf between its claims and reality, and also within an art scene which, until these artists made their appearance, used to pay tribute to a totalitarian form of aestheticism. When they revived the conventional techniques of frescoes, oil paintings, watercolours, drawings, mosaics, stone and bronze sculptures, it was more than just a protest by the younger against the older generation which had proclaimed the end of painting. It was also the only way in which the artists could define their egos by artistic means. Photography, film and video, the meagre materials of *arte povera*, seemed repulsive to many artists whose imagination demanded more sensuality. They were instruments which simply resisted any attempt to employ them for the direct expression of emotions. Without a carefully planned concept, they cannot be used at

Mimmo Paladino:
Untitled, 1982
Oil on canvas, 78¾ × 118⅛ in.
(200 × 300 cm)
Nationalgalerie, West Berlin

all, so that they dampen any artistic passion. As a result, there was an artistic explosion of Informal Art, inspired by the Surrealist *écriture automatique* which, in turn, had been influenced by the therapeutic findings of psychoanalysis, and this explosion loosened the stylistic fetters on painting. Suddenly the art of painting – a medium which had been declared dead – seemed to become the most suitable vehicle for the unrestrained artistic urge of a whole generation of artists who had been born around the year 1940. "After all, one must not forget that this art is also concerned with establishing a direct link between the subject (i.e. the artist with all his yearnings, desires, dreams and fantasies) and the object (the material result, i.e. the picture, drawing, etc). The physical act of painting, the way in which the artist uses his brush or pencil, express his spontaneous desire to carry out an idea immediately, to give shape to an image, so that they can bear the artist's sensory perception." (Zdenek Felix) At first many of the artists still used the traditional media in the manner of *arte povera*. This could be seen in a number of works by Italian artists, shown at the Stuttgart exhibition *Europe 79*. But there were already signs of a radical change, and an accomplished painter like Chia, well-versed in the history of 20th century art, had already begun to put it into practice. In his

Enzo Cucchi:
Untitled, 1985
Oil and pencil on canvas,
110¼ × 126 in. (280 × 320 cm)
Galerie Bernd Klüser, Munich

paintings Chia enforces a synthesis of tradition and modernity, he creates diagrams in which non-simultaneous phenomena are shown as being simultaneous, and achieves highly ambivalent messages, without eliminating the contradictions that are emphasized. However, he does not always avoid the dangers of a dull Neo-Classicism with gaudy decorations, and in his mature paintings of the mid-eighties he tends to revel in an exuberant, luxurious, but at the same time rather lightweight, decorativeness. He did not retain the subversive eclecticism of his early paintings, but hedged his bets by making his works easier to recognize – which certainly made them more marketable.

Cucchi's art seems to concentrate more on aspects that are directly connected with art itself, which does not mean, however, that his works did not sell. His paintings have a mysterious quality about them, and their sombre aura, sometimes reminiscent of Kiefer's paintings, also suggests apocalyptic images. The use of colours that are almost black, and the occasional flicker of glowing red or glaring reddish-yellow, like the still hot embers of a dying world – these are elements which fulfil a very concrete, sensual purpose. Like Kiefer, Cucchi occasionally extends the space within the painting to make it three-dimensional, thus giving it an unsettling presence which almost physically attacks the viewer. "The space of the canvas or paper does not act as the basis of the painting, but is full of radiance itself, thus turning it into a source of energy. The basic idea is that of an art which is rooted in the material world and which establishes a chain of contacts and flexible relationships between objects. This even reaches the point where objects become signs that indicate a different position altogether, a dynamic reference point, where high and low come together." (Bonito Oliva)

Clemente is the most complex artist among the *Transavantguardia* painters. His paintings

Sandro Chia:
Blue Grotto, 1980
Grotta Azzurra
Oil on canvas, 57⅞ × 81⅞ in.
(147 × 208 cm)
Sammlung Bruno Bischofberger, Zurich
Küsnacht

are often based on incidents in his own life. He has painted a number of self-portraits in which he focuses on the way he looks at someone who is looking at him. Clemente contributed four paintings to the *Zeitgeist* exhibition in Berlin, which had been organized by Christos M. Joachimidis and Norman Rosenthal. It was a powerful demonstration of the post-avant-garde and indeed its eventual triumph. Three of Clemente's paintings bore the rather indicative titles *My House*, *My Parents* and *My Travels*. He continuously changes his artistic identity, with the exception of a small number of formal stereotypes which he has left unchanged and which could therefore be understood as a kind of trademark. His method of structuring his paintings avoids structural clarity, with a permanent change of identity in what should be unmistakably either three- or two-dimensional space. His painting *My House*, for instance, which is reminiscent of Kiefer's "attic paintings", shows the cross-section of a two-storey building, with a typical middle-class sitting-room on the ground floor and a hall with supporting columns on the upper floor, accessible by a winding staircase. As in real life, the floor of the columned hall is also the ceiling of the sitting-room. However, this cannot really be depicted in a painting, unless it is shown in the form of a rhomboid area which, like an optical illusion, constantly changes from one state to another. Naturalist elements can be found side by side with the decorative, the banal and even with elements of serious art. An additional, two-dimensional structure alternates with an illusionist style of composition, and the mythical past meets with the present. Clemente's programme is that of total eclecticism, and his art

cannot be fully defined. It has the iridescence and strangeness of Parmigianino, that great Mannerist. Even his artistic attitude is reminiscent of his Mannerist forerunners. Clemente strictly rejects any interpretation of his art. It is significant that even his admirers say that he does not have any messages. The focal point of Clemente's art is his ego: he is a solipsist, who believes that all reality is subjective, not a self-indulgent narcissist. His paintings and drawings are the areas onto which he projects his own psychological obsessions, with a remote echo of the psychopathology of Mannerism. After all, were not the strangest stories told about Mannerist painters, too? Indeed, there was hardly anyone among them who led a normal life, and the state of their minds suggested that they were the first artists of a modern type.

"What interests me – not just in art – is everything mysterious, unexplored and forgotten," Paladino said on one occasion, a confession with which he brought yet another element of Mannerist aspirations into play. Among this Italian *squadra*, Paladino is the one who most enjoys experimenting, although his career has never had the same fairy-tale quality as the three *big C's*. Quite apart from the fact that intrigues made it difficult for him to reach the dizzier heights of the art market, Paladino chose the most difficult artistic path. He has always been driven by a burning curiosity – a cross between a cat and a witch is a major motif in one of his earlier paintings – and this inquisitiveness has led Paladino along a path which involves quite a few artistic risks. Unlike Clemente, he leaves his artistic ego out. The only way in

Enzo Cucchi:
Enchanted City, 1986
Città Incantata
Oil on canvas, lead and iron,
94½ × 275½ in. (240 × 700 cm)
Galerie Bernd Klüser, Munich

95

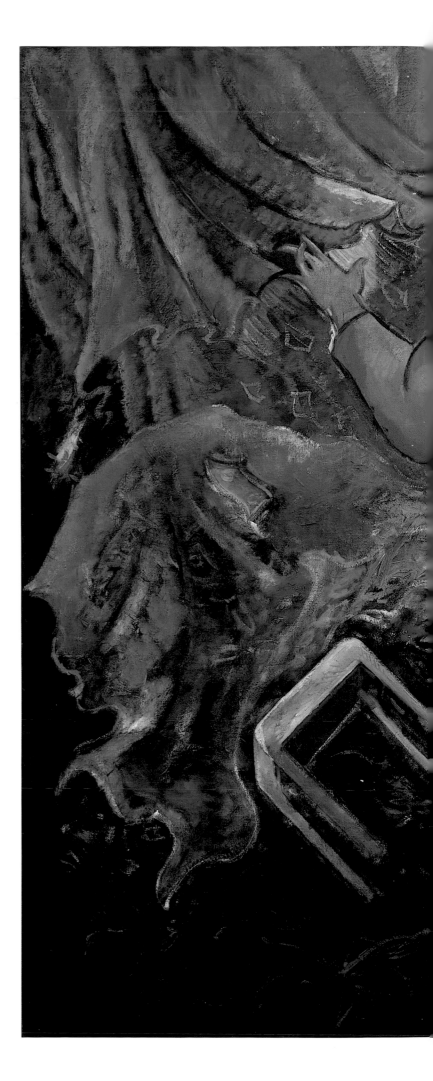

Sandro Chia:
Incident at the Tintoretto Café, 1982
Successo al Caffè Tintoretto
Oil on canvas, 88⅛ × 130 in.
(225 × 330 cm)
Sammlung Bruno Bischofberger, Zurich
Küsnacht

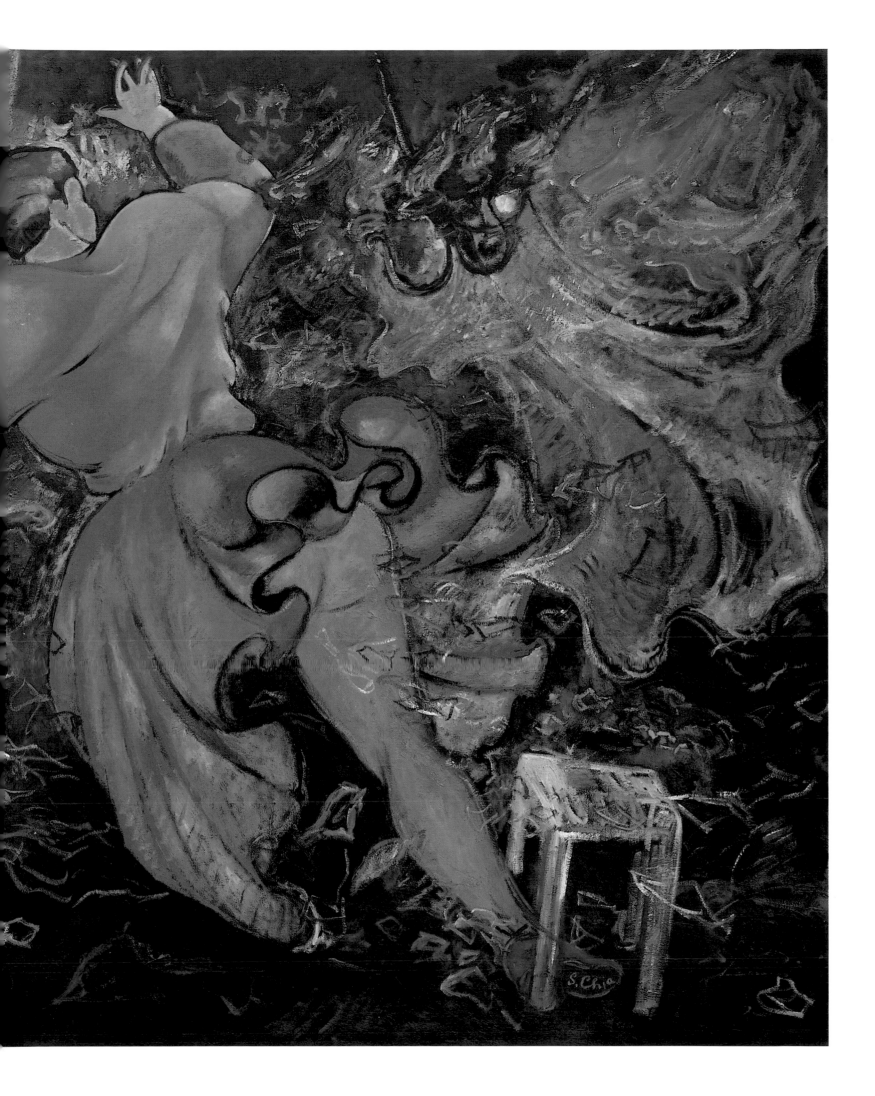

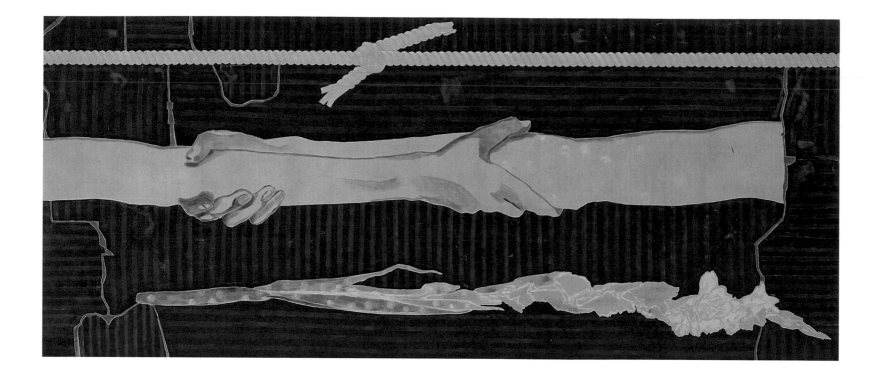

Francesco Clemente:
Alpine Grip, 1987
Coloured pigment on canvas,
73⅜ × 183 in. (187 × 465 cm)
Sammlung Bruno Bischofberger, Zurich
Küsnacht

which it manifests itself is in his very personal choice of subjects and themes. Beginning with schematic abstraction in the spirit of Paul Klee and Wassily Kandinsky, i.e. the kind that could still be seen at the *Europe 79* exhibition, his artistic ideas unfolded in the form of mosaic maps which are figurative, full of metaphors and rich in colour. With daring compositions that contradict our ingrained habits of vision, both the space and the plane of these paintings invoke a mild sense of insecurity in the viewer. The reaction which takes hold of us when we look at his paintings is described more accurately in Italian: the viewer is seized by a sense of *grande instabilità*, a feeling that takes hold of him very gradually. The artistic sledgehammer is not one of Paladino's tools. Instead, his methods are characterized by a degree of subtlety that is full of allusions. Paladino appeals to the intellect and the emotions, which probably makes him the most authentic Italian among *Transavantguardia* artists. But even Paladino seeks those borderline areas in his art which are close to intellectual reasoning. He places his top-heavy figures against fiery red or yellowish ochre backgrounds, thus conjuring up associations of prehistoric cave painting. In the mid-eighties he began to indicate the space within a painting by means of colour, and whenever he drew any contours at all, it was merely to sketch his figures, together with a few typical features and attributes. This is particularly apparent in the characteristic heads which dominate a large number of his paintings and which partly rage amongst a turmoil of chaos – ambiguous ciphers, half human, half skulls. His work is filled with mysteries and puzzles, but they are not unclear. What is more, Paladino admits his artistic errors, and his unsuccessful mosaics, which he had shown at the Paris Biennial in 1985, were missing from the Munich retrospective of the same year.

We need only glance at the cultural history of the sixteenth century, and particularly the history of different "mentalities", to see that the relationship between Mannerism and post-avant-garde art, especially in its Italian version, is anything but superficial. It was then that man began to lose his faith in the unity between himself and his environment, and he gradually became aware of his deeply rooted lack of continuity. This awareness was the price he had to pay for his ability to develop. He detached himself from the world around him and confronted it as an active agent, fully responsible for his own actions. The discovery and perfection of the central perspective in painting provides a vivid illustration of man's process of distancing himself: it was tantamount to a second, self-imposed expulsion from paradise. Gradually man lost the feeling of being part of his natural environment, and in time he learnt to dominate it. The world became concrete and objective. "This process in which reality becomes unreal – which we can also call "alienation" or "decentration" if we want to use different terminology – manifests itself above all in the way we experience our modern age as a historical period. Unlike in Graeco-Roman times, man's identity is no longer supported by a

Francesco Clemente:
Suonno, 1982
Water-colour on paper, 85 × 34⅞ in.
(216 × 88.5 cm)
Sammlung Bruno Bischofberger, Zurich
Küsnacht

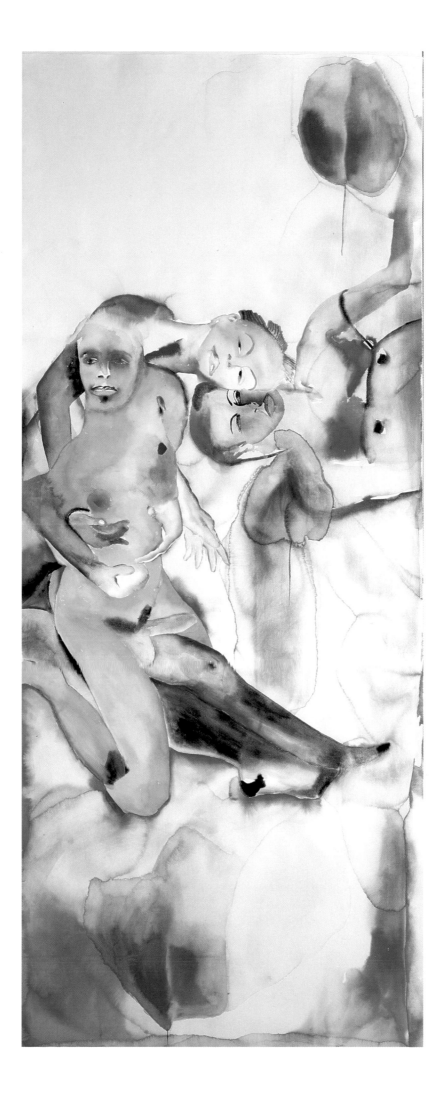

Francesco Clemente:
Tender Lie, 1984
Mixed media on wood and aluminium,
21 × 29 in. (53.5 × 66.1 cm)
Sammlung Bruno Bischofberger, Zurich
Küsnacht

number of different gods, nor is it caused by one God, as was believed in the Middle Ages. But after the age of Theodicy and with the advent of the Enlightenment, modern man now has to be fully and solely responsible for finding his own identity. It is something that is no longer taken for granted, but has become a problem which needs solving." (Japp)

These findings by a literary scholar are matched by a hypothesis put forward by the Austrian art historian Werner Hofmann. He maintains that modern art began with Martin Luther's statement that art was neither good nor evil. Visual images, said Luther, "are neutral with regard to morality and religion, and unlike the word and the sacrament, they are not partly essential." He thus denied any power that a work of art might have, so that the decision as to whether it was good or evil became entirely the responsibility of the individual. Evil, said Luther, "lies within the individual who invokes it, not in the work of art itself." Hofmann concluded from then onwards it was the beholder who had to decide the meaning of a painting. As a result, the same gulf began to open between art and the viewer as between reality and man. Hofmann then goes on to quote the philosopher Hegel: "One may indeed hope that art will continue to improve and perfect itself, but its form has ceased to be the highest aim of the human mind. No matter how excellent we may find the images of the Greek

Gérard Garouste:
Columbia, 1981
Oil on canvas, 98¾ × 116 in.
(250.8 × 294.6 cm)
Leo Castelli Gallery, New York

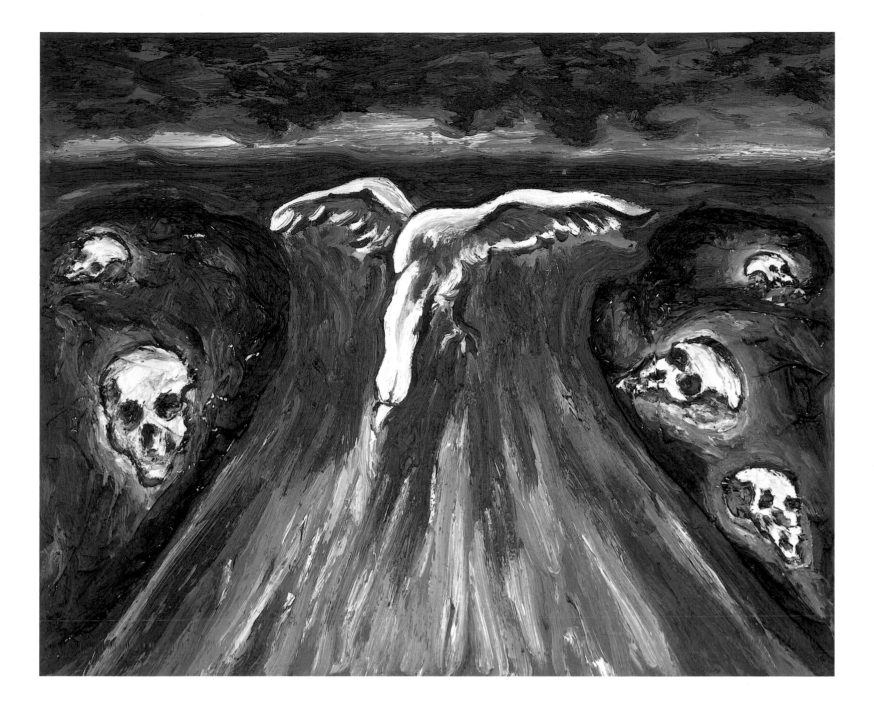

gods or how dignified and perfect the renderings of God the Father or Christ or Mary – it is useless because we will no longer kneel down before them."

Hofmann does not see this as the end of art, but rather the beginning of a critical attitude towards it. A closer look at Mannerist paintings reveals that they are filled with a deep feeling of unrest. Consider the intensity of the passions that are expressed in the glass-like bodies of Bronzino, the depth of mute despair which comes to the surface in Giovanni Battista Rosso's winding groups of snake-like figures, and the immense horror that emanates from the great paintings by Tintoretto and El Greco. Not to mention the festive exuberance and unrestrained sexuality of Giulio Romano's engravings, which became known as *Aretino's Positions*. These are only known to us as copies of the original, because the plates were destroyed at the order of the Pope himself.

Does this mean that Mannerism and post-avant-garde mark the beginning and the end of what is commonly known as the Modern Age – a period with an uncertain outcome? It is true that the affinities between the two are very striking, but it would be wrong to ignore the differences. The world has become smaller, and the post-avant-garde includes an element of cosmopolitanism which was completely lacking in Mannerism. However, an even more important difference is the note of irony, which has been one of the driving forces of the post-avant-garde. Without this ironical distance it would be no more than a poor imitation. But

Enzo Cucchi:
Uncultivated Landscape, 1983
Paesaggio Barbaro
Oil on canvas, 51 × 62¾ in.
(129.5 × 159.4 cm)
Angela Westwater Collection, New York

103

how does this irony show? In literature, this question can be answered quite easily. Literature is the attempt to comprehend the world by means of language, so that on a literary level irony can be regarded as the contradiction of this attempt. Loosely, the ironical person says the opposite of what he means. Now, in the area of visual arts things are somewhat different. Indeed, it is in the very nature of art that a painter cannot depict an object in two different ways at the same time. He paints a person as either beautiful or ugly. On the other hand, it is possible to paint an ordinary person in the same way that kings, potentates and archbishops have traditionally been portrayed. In doing so the artist exalts the ordinary person, while at the same time undermining the mode of expression which used to be reserved for those in high places. There is something unmistakably subversive in such an approach, because the artist has devalued an artistic model which is an expression of social power. The artist operates on the level of artistic form, and this is true not only for portraits, but also for numerous other visual forms. As soon as an artistic movement or style has become the norm, it will try to consolidate its position and extend its sphere of influence. It becomes a dominant power that sets strict standards. However, the autocratic power of such a movement is always limited, because people begin to resist it, either openly or secretly.

The avant-garde revolted quite openly against the omnipotence of 19th-century academic art and finally emerged victorious. But what has been far more common in the history of art is a strategy of secret attacks and subversive gibes. The art historian Richard Hamann described an example of this during the Golden Age of Dutch Paintings: "The revolution (of the Dutch – K.H.) was directed above all against the art of the princely courts, and – like 15th century art or the time of Dürer – this meant the secularization of pictures of saints by satirizing them and dragging them down to a common, worldly level. The first phase might be called Baroque not only because the subjects themselves were Baroque – i.e. turned back to front and dragged down to a lower level of humanity – but also the revolutionary compositions, which were aimed at the general public and whose language was as loud and noisy as the propaganda of the sacred paintings. Nevertheless, Baroque art does not recommend anything, but seeks to offend. It is not enticing, only challenging. Its proclamations are like the fiery speeches of a revolutionary, and these are not just *for* something, but also *against* the subjects which had been rendered divine in Baroque art."

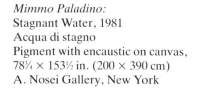

Mimmo Paladino:
Stagnant Water, 1981
Acqua di stagno
Pigment with encaustic on canvas,
78¾ × 153½ in. (200 × 390 cm)
A. Nosei Gallery, New York

What is important here is the question of how such a "revolution" occurs in art. Hamann mentions satire as one of the most widespread methods. Others are travesty and caricature, including graffiti. When Lanigan-Schmidt, for instance, builds an altar consisting of consumer goods, he employs the means of travesty. Travesty is the clashing of two incompatible spheres. In Lanigan-Schmidt's example, it was the sphere of the sacred and the profane: the profane has parked itself squarely in the sacred sphere and has simply adapted its aura. And when Chia paints his human figures as if they were inflated rubber dolls, then he is using the method of caricature, distorting the familiar and giving special emphasis to those elements which he wants to stand out. Satire, travesty and caricature are artistic methods which are not only legitimate but also very common. They express more than just the modest desire to give us a good laugh and therefore make us feel freer. Let us make no mistake: they are above all artistic tools of irony, and even in that much-quoted emphasis on the figurative, which is so typical of the Italian *Transavantguardia*, irony is at work. This emphasis can only ever be experienced as a loss, and this loss is the theme of Chia's "physical" paintings and sculptures. The exaggerated images of Chia's bulging hulks suggest regret at the loss of genuine sensuality in everyday life. When a person is in a dark cellar, he whistles out loud to dispel his fear, and this ironical ambiguity is frequently found in post-avant-garde art. With the concept of irony we can also explain the complex relationship between avant-garde and post-avant-garde. Indeed, there is a good deal of irony in the fact that the art of the eighties can best be described as "new", yet wearing the cloak of an earlier artistic trend.

Salvo:
Eight Books, 1983
8 Libri
Oil on wood, 20½ × 27⅛ in.
(52 × 69 cm)
Galerie Paul Maenz, Cologne

The Cultural Supermarket

The Italian artists soon met with responses in other countries. In West Germany it was Baselitz, Lüpertz, Immendorff and Kiefer who had given painting a new image. Beuys had shifted the narrow confines of the avant-garde far beyond the spheres of art, and American mass culture had at times fired the imagination of artists considerably more than the barren objects of avant-garde art. Dahn and Dokoupil tested photocopying methods for their artistic suitability. Polaroid photography became popular, and a number of artists enjoyed using this medium for private erotic pleasure. It seemed at first as if the new figurative awareness of the Italians had the most lasting influence on German artists. The first *Mülheimer Freiheit* paintings showed that the painters revelled in this. But physical themes were also emphasized in Berlin, where figurative art had never been pushed into a minor role and where painters like Hödicke and Bernd Koberling had already initiated a slightly more Expressionist revival. There was Rainer Fetting's impressive series of *Shower Paintings*, his *American Indian* series and his *Mirror Paintings*, there were Helmut Middendorf's iridescent paintings about the music scene with their hammering rhythms, the ghost-like rendering of Berlin's nocturnal skyline, its unsettling deep-blue sky without any lights, Salomé's *Swimmers* and Elvira Bach's strong women. These Berlin painters had derived their inspiration from the world in which they moved. A narcissistic element is unmistakable in their art, whereas motifs from art history are less frequent. When they do occur, they are turned "back to front", i.e. as travesties or parodies. In his painting *Crucifixion* (1982) it is not Christ but his own body which Fetting has nailed to the cross, and instead of the traditional mourning disciples and Mary, he is surrounded by a gigantic skull, inflated out of all proportion. And the eagle in *Strange Feathers* (1983) by Ina Barfuss is losing its tail feathers after enjoying a good bite from Prometheus' liver. Instead, the feathers are now sprouting from the Titan's posterior.

It is not a uniform style or a uniform direction which unites these artists, but a common age and similar experiences in their lives. The works of the Berlin artists seem to be the most conventional ones. They were inspired by Kirchner's paintings of big cities and the stern, serious paintings by Hödicke, who taught and influenced some of the artists. The most daringly experimental painters were the artists from the Rhineland, with their breathtaking romps through the various genres and their obvious citations from popular culture. The Hamburg artists – Werner Büttner and the two brothers, Albert and Markus Oehlen – lie between these two positions. But such regional differences tell us little; and in any case the artists travel a good deal. German artists prefer to live and work wherever they can find favourable opportunities. They feel attracted by cultural climates that are emotionally charged, such as Berlin with its special position, or Cologne with its varied Rhineland scene. It is indicative that, at least in the early paintings, they were particularly fond of sombre and dirty colours. Büttner, the Oehlen brothers, Ina Barfuss, Wachweger, and at times Dahn excel in these shades, which Büttner said he found really "beautiful". There is also an element of protest against the highly polished hotch-potch aestheticism of advertising and T.V. commercials which have, as it were, robbed the sensual element of its physical impact. It is the "filth" of everyday life which gives these paintings a dimension of vitality.

When we look at the first paintings of this movement, we can discern an instinctive longing, a desire for contact, touch, warmth and direct physical experience. This aspect of the subject

Walter Dahn:
Victory of Good over Evil (News from H.U.B.), 1986
Das Gute siegt (Nachricht von H.U.B.)
Acrylic on canvas, 118⅛ × 78¾ in.
(300 × 200 cm)
Galerie Paul Maenz, Cologne

Walter Dahn:
Asthma I, 1982
Dispersion on muslin, 78¾ × 59 in.
(200 × 150 cm)
Private collection

Peter Bömmels:
Leap from History, 1982
Sprung aus der Geschichte
Dispersion and gold bronze on muslin,
86⅝ × 126 in. (220 × 320 cm)
Galerie Paul Maenz, Cologne

Page 110:

Rainer Fetting:
Man under the Shower IV, 1981/82
Mann in Dusche IV
Dispersion on canvas, 98½ × 63 in.
(250 × 160 cm)
Private collection, Cologne

Page 111:

Salomé:
Zeitgeist IV, 1982
Synthetic resin on muslin,
157½ × 118⅛ in. (400 × 300 cm)

matter is matched by the images. The physical element is almost orgiastic. The paintings are full of copulating couples, masturbation, crapping, puking, strangling and beating, torturing and beheading. By showing the world as distorted, fragmented, battered, and usually inhabited by grimacing figures, these artists re-invest it with a physical impact. Dahn and Dokoupil have been splitting the skulls of robots as well as those of their own self-portraits. But it is irrelevant whether it is a robot or a human being who is being maltreated in such a way; the pain has an immediate effect on the viewer. The scenes in the paintings are garishly illuminated, the subjects are roughly painted, the paintings are dominated by caricature and the grotesque, and one can feel the penetrating, shrill sound of rock music. The beautiful, cool world of Minimal and Concept Art seems to have been bombed by this sort of art. Avant-garde art had become as sterile as the academic art which it had once ousted, and had turned into something academic itself.

With the exception of Büttner and Bömmels, none of the artists were self-taught, but they had all been students of less eminent art schools, rather than the fortress of avant-garde theory, the academy in Düsseldorf.

The art of these young painters in the early eighties was quite deliberately "primitive" and consciously artless, although it must be said that this intended primitiveness also had a satirical function, i.e. that of parody and a "filthy" reversal of the "hollow forms" of the avant-garde. So it is, in a sense, well within the continuous process of artistic development. The open violence of these paintings, their seeming or genuine artlessness and undisguised sexuality clearly support the material side of existence, thus spitting against the idealistic wind of respectable art. "The material element, the fully alert body, actively proves its sovereignty. The vulgar, which has so far been excluded, enters into the marketplace and demonstratively challenges the sublime. Faeces, urine and sperm! It is a matter of 'vegetating' like a dog, and

Walter Dahn:
Crystal Morning, 1983
Kristallmorgen
Dispersion on muslin, 70⅞ × 59 in.
Schürmann Collection, Herzogenrath

yet living, laughing and giving the impression that behind all this stands not confusion, but clear reflection." (Peter Sloterdijk)

Dahn's work, in particular, is in many ways quite symptomatic of the art of the eighties. While Beuys made the greatest impression on him, his time with Polke at his farmhouse in Willich was also influential. Dahn, who often cooperates closely with his friend Dokoupil, is one of the most Protean figures in contemporary German art. Before he turned to painting, he used to explore modern reproduction techniques. And after several years of painting – and a simultaneous interest in video and music – he produced a remarkable series of photographic works. Dahn always plans his paintings, and sometimes also his photographs, by means of numerous drawings. The subject matter in his drawings constantly varies, and it is a choice which is mainly inspired by the "vulgar language of the street." (Charles Jencks) Neither Dahn's nor Dokoupil's paintings can be called "savage". Although the specific theme of a painting is always based on a spontaneous idea, the actual production process shows that Dahn constantly checks and re-checks, changes and re-formulates.

Dahn enjoys using cartoon-like exaggeration. In one painting a fist can be seen jerking forward from a dark background, illuminating, as it were, the viewer with a candle in its fingers. A drunkard is holding his head in his hands so that the bottle at his neck can empty more quickly. A chain-smoker consists of a clamp with a string of burning cigarettes, with the second asthma attack holding a skull in its arms. And an Italian painter living in Switzerland reminds us of a Chinese Buddha. Dahn's paintings throw the viewer into a state of insecurity. The artist seems fully aware of the conceptual background of his art, thus emphasizing that his art is not mindless. Dahn countered the accusations that he could not paint with a series of delicate paintings, with subtle shades and a restrained subject matter. The paradoxical breaches in his art are the result of a rigorous re-appraisal of traditional artistic values, a

Top left:

Ina Barfuss:
Sacrificial Gift (of the Self to the Id), 1986
Opfergabe (vom Selbst zum Es)
Oil on canvas, 59 × 43⅜ in.
(150 × 110 cm)

Top right:

Thomas Wachweger:
Evacuation Plan, 1986
Evakuierungsplan
Indian ink on paper and canvas,
82¾ × 59 in. (210 × 150 cm)
Hamburg, Produzentengalerie Hamburg

Page 113:

Markus Oehlen:
Landscape, 1987
Landschaft
Oil on canvas, 78¾ × 59 in.
(200 × 150 cm)
Galerie Max Hetzler, Cologne

Walter Dahn:
Self, Twice, 1982
Selbst Doppelt
Dispersion on canvas, 78¾ × 90½ in.
(200 × 250 cm)
Private collection

LÖSCHT MIT BLUT DAS BRENNENDE WISSE

process in which artistic forms were consistently used with irony. There is a quality of ironical solemnity about his paintings – profane travesties, full of romantic sorrow, that tell us about obvious loss.

Dahn pursues the most diverse ideas. Some of his drawings and paintings are based on photographs from ethnological catalogues, and in his photo-pieces he makes use of photographic prints from magazines as well as his own snaps of interesting street scenes. The way in which he uses photography as a medium is symptomatic. Again and again he changes the originals by means of the most diverse printing techniques, sometimes using colour, or duplicating black-and-white negatives, or trying various different lighting effects. The resulting painting is never a final version. Dahn gets his ideas from museums as well as from the streets, from graffiti, from gigantic advertising posters, and from city life. He takes photos of his friends and people in the art world, and his friend Dokoupil once painted a gallery of such portraits.

For post-avant-garde art it makes very little difference where the ideas originally came from. In his enticing series of *Blue Paintings about Love* (1982) Dokoupil took the trademarks of a number of market leaders and re-modelled them into his own eccentric sculptures with fashionable colours. Most notable was the Omo Gate at Sonsbeek Park in Holland (1986) – a late capitalist triumphal arch, made of plastic, in the middle of a little wood near a small village – a macabre joke which hits you right between the eyes, an artistic travesty that could

Jiri Georg Dokoupil:
The Studio, 1984
Das Atelier
Acrylic on canvas, 45 × 57½ in.
114 × 146 cm
Private collection, Amsterdam

Hans-Peter Adamski:
Hiroshima, 1981
Dispersion on canvas, 86⅝ × 63 in.
(220 × 160 cm)

116

Helmut Middendorf:
Singer IV, 1981
Sänger IV
Synthetic resin on muslin,
74¾ × 90½ in. (190 × 230 cm)
Jung Collection, Aachen

Page 119:

Elvira Bach:
Untitled, 1985
Dispersion on canvas, 65 × 51¼ in.
(165 × 130 cm)
Karl Pfefferle Galerie & Edition, Munich

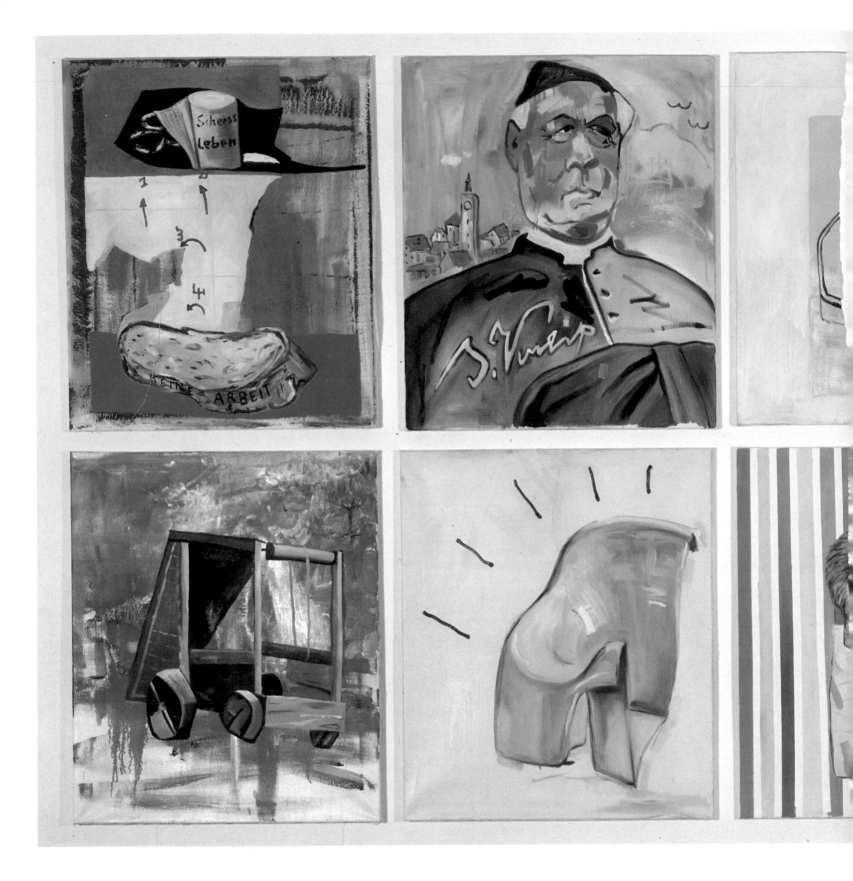

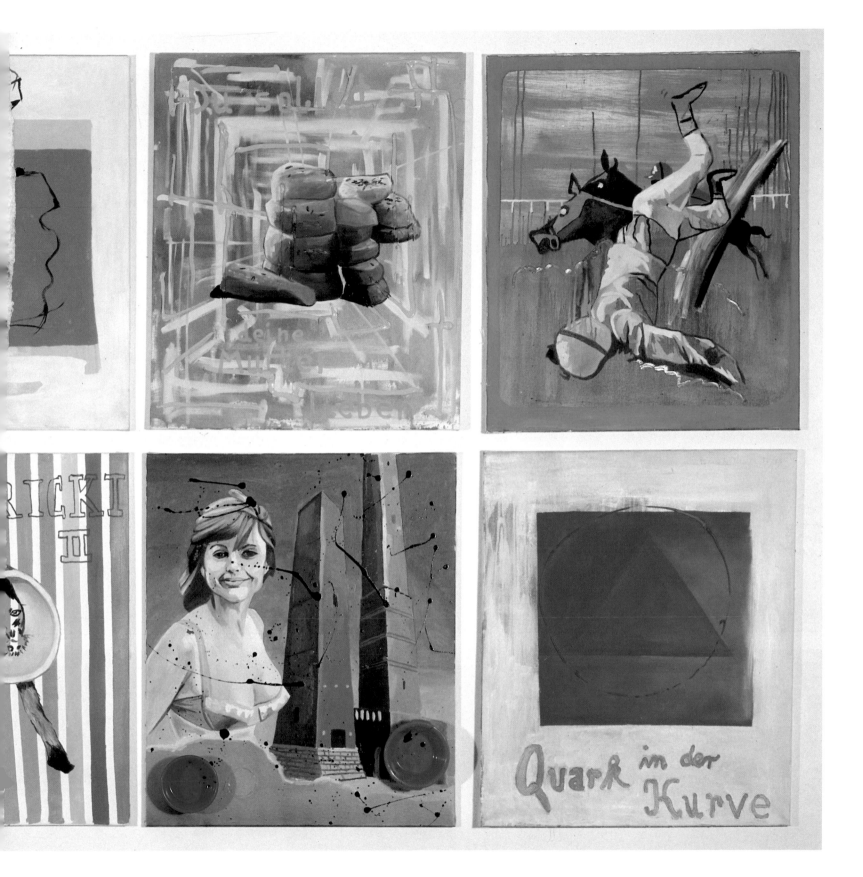

Martin Kippenberger:
Buggered for Ideas, 1982/3
(1) Life is crap – no work 1 Seek 2 and 3 ye shall 4 find – Jesus
(2) Fatso (3) I Could Have Told You (4) The Smelly Cheese Family
(5) Typical of Gravity (Physics We Can Understand)
(6) Predecessor of Capri (7) Section of a Child's Potty as Designed by Colani
(8) Ricki II (9) Tits, Towers, Tortellini
(10) I Wouldn't Have Minded If You'd Meant Me
Mixed media on canvas, ten pieces, 35½ × 29½ in. (90 × 75 cm) each
Private collection, New York

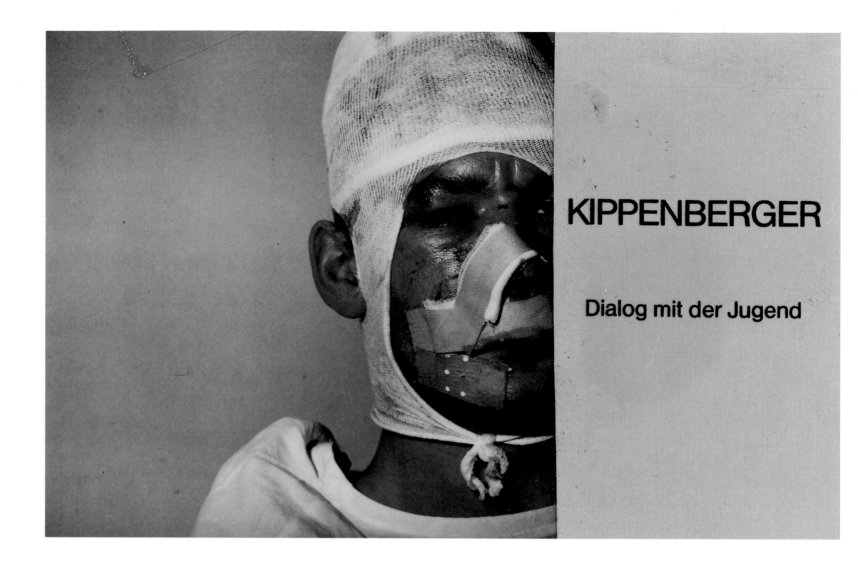

KIPPENBERGER

Dialog mit der Jugend

not have been more pungent. For his first solo exhibition at a museum – the Folkwang Museum in Essen – he published a gilt-edged catalogue that looked like a prayer book, with texts written by friends. This was meant as a bold parody of the majority of catalogues, which tend to be full of bombastic pomp and empty phrases.

Dokoupil is a virtuoso of a painter and a never-ending source of bright ideas. The most disparate spheres mingle in his subject matter, and – like his fellow-artists – he uses a strategy of artistic satire and subversion to meet the visual challenges that constantly surround him. His *Studies of a New Image of Man* present flat figures in dirty pink against a dark background, distorted like the figures in Mannerist art. A painting called *Documenta Contribution No.I* satirizes the title of a famous work of art by Beuys. His *Theoretical Paintings* are captivatingly painted paraphrases of abstract paintings in museums with nonsensical or filthy titles. A number of his *Terry-Cloth Paintings* close the famous Lucio Fontana slit with a zip. And in his *Dummy Paintings* (American: Pacifier Paintings) all kinds of motifs are shown against a night-blue background and, as suggested in the title, each painting includes a brightly illuminated orange rubber dummy (pacifier). It is pointless to try and follow Dokoupil's artistic tracks. One would only be led astray, which is precisely what the artist intends. As Jean Christophe Amman confessed in a catalogue, no artist in recent years had confused and irritated him as much as Dokoupil.

Bömmels, Adamski, Kever and Naschberger – another four *Mülheimer Freiheit* musketeers – developed their own individual style within the framework of post-avant-garde art, less Protean than Dokoupil's works, but with equally surprising variety. Bömmels' twisted figures, composed of small particles, symbolize a permanent state of change and fluid transience. He does not think much of superficial jokes, and the horror which sometimes emanates from his paintings affects us with a directness that lacks all alienating distance. Bömmels, who like Büttner is self-taught, sees the work of an artist as a task of self-

inspection. No sooner had he mastered the craft of painting, than he began to produce reliefs, using the characteristic motifs of his art; at one point, he also spent over a year trying his hand at sculpting, in order to produce a red sandstone frieze, consisting of many different parts.

If Bömmels' paintings and sculptures are still relatively easy to identify, the only recognizable feature of Hans-Peter Adamski's art is its lack of identity. There is no clear style, no theme that he repeatedly enlarges upon, no particular medium or material which he prefers. The artist refuses to be pinpointed. It is the irony of someone who seeks refuge in the alienation between the world and art, but is equally addicted to both. His artistic truth consists of many truths, and he categorically rejects any claim to an all-encompassing truth. Instead of an exhaustive exegesis, he included a comprehensive introduction to *Aquaristics* in his first major catalogue. Adamski, the oldest of the *Mülheimer Freiheit* artists, has remained an outsider of the art world, similar in his aspirations to Richter. Like the other Mülheimers, though, he ardently tries to free art of all fetters of doctrine. Gerard Kever and Gerhard Naschberger fit into this group of unorthodox artists, even though they never quite attained the same degree of significance.

But who is Martin Kippenberger? To say that he is an artist only answers the easiest part of the question. Even a detailed description of his art is rather difficult. A few years ago a Hamburg newspaper printed Kippenberger's own brief description of himself: "A spendthrift, animator, showman, a show-off, ring-leader, and compère." What is certainly true is that Kippenberger is primarily concerned with unmasking all the falsehood and pretentiousness that surrounds our human existence. He has spent some time in Berlin where he became friends with Büttner. He has organized exhibitions and bought paintings. He pretends to be happy-go-lucky, and yet he is the exact opposite. Kippenberger is a gambler, and he gambles above all with the false expectations which people have when he assumes different roles. Obviously, however, his way of acting the artist does not correspond to the

Top left:

Martin Kippenberger:
Not Knowing Why, But Knowing What For, 1984
Nicht wissen warum, aber wissen wozu
Oil on canvas, 63 × 51⅛ in.
(160 × 130 cm)
Schürmann Collection, Herzogenrath

Top right:

Martin Kippenberger: Nice Communist Girl, 1983
Sympathische Kommunistin
Oil on canvas, 47¼ × 39⅜ in.
(120 × 100 cm)
Private collection

Page 124:

Albert Oehlen:
By the Tree, 1984
Am Baum
Oil on canvas, 74¾ × 63 in.
(190 × 160 cm)
Private collection, Cologne

Page 125:

Albert Oehlen:
Untitled, 1982
Oil and varnish on canvas,
98½ × 78¾ in. (250 × 200 cm)

predominant ideas of what an artist should be. His behaviour and attitudes are part and parcel of a definite social and cultural environment from which they derive their impetus and at which his art is aimed. Kippenberger is an artist with "the evil eye", and the reality at which he directs his eye is often madder than any artist's imagination might conceive. His "repertoire", as he calls it, confronts this reality, adjusts itself to it and changes it beyond recognition with artistic methods until it becomes recognizable again, following Bertolt Brecht's maxim. If his paintings and series of paintings appear to be distorted, then that is nothing but the effect of a mirror which straightens out its images, "without mystifying the past or beautifying the future." (Wilfried W. Dickhoff) This does not mean that the artist has lost his grip on himself. He may share Dokoupil's irony, but it is not an irony which creates a distance or unmasks anything. Kippenberger is right in the thick of the world to which he holds up his distorting mirror. He has a lot in common with Dahn and Adamski, and also with Polke. He is a post-avant-garde artist, but not a Post-Modern one.

Kippenberger's "repertoire" owes its allegiance to the concept of enlightenment, which makes it modern and thus almost (still) avant-garde. He lacks the self-infatuation of a Narcissus and the irresponsible attitude of a hedonist, even though he very much enjoys striking such a pose. His painting *War – Wicked* (1983) shows a warship with its cannon raised in a rather threatening way; underneath the cannon there is a Father Christmas holding a switch (for naughty children). This scene is set against the background of a yellow sea and a threatening blue sky. A ridiculous combination? Kippenberger takes the clichés of the politicians, of mass-produced photographs and of advertising, and uses them in a literal way. As soon as it becomes necessary to blind people's eyes to an acute threat to our existence, and when those who are supposedly in control make their speeches, there is indeed something ridiculous about the hollow phrases and attempts to soothe the public. War, nuclear power, chemicals, carbon dioxide, street fights – wicked! A *Dialogue with the Young* (1984) has had painful consequences: a self-portrait shows a photograph of the artist with a thick bandage round his head; he had ended up in hospital. The titles of Kippenberger's paintings are as important as the paintings themselves, because they reinforce each other. The artist grabs his themes from the pile of images in our modern mass society, often contrasting them with respectable art. His method, too, is that of travesty: the actress Julie Christie, who acted in the famous screen epic *Doctor Zhivago*, appears side by side with a painting in the style of Paul Bonnard or one of Kippenberger's own paintings. He has painted them all and distorted them, turning them into components of a ten-part series, with the title *Whatever Happened on a Sunday?* (1982). A scene from everyday life in a petty bourgeois culture.

Kippenberger cooperates very closely with Albert Oehlen and Werner Büttner. He and Oehlen often give provocative performances, some of which quite frequently end in fights. The texts are usually their own, nonsensical sentences, stuck together with no more than an appearance of logic, and their meaning is never completely clear. Nevertheless, the easy-going way in which these verbal structures are handled occasionally reveals a flash of deep despair, even though this despair is often well hidden below a layer of insolence. Herold – who is forever crossing the border between avant-garde and post-avant-garde art – and Büttner create madly twisted sculptures out of ordinary materials such as crossbars, bricks, wire and discarded everyday objects, whereas Kippenberger and Oehlen pile up whole cascades of sentences, which the gluttonous digestive system of the art market obviously finds rather difficult to process. Oehlen, incidentally, is one of the most interesting painters in the German art world. Unlike the Berlin artists, he did not yield to the torrential maelstrom which broke out so suddenly. Rather, he has been subjecting his art to a constant process of checking and re-checking, often together with Büttner. Oehlen began to paint relatively late, and it was his brother Markus who first encouraged him. It is only in a very ironical sense that Oehlen and Büttner regard themselves as artists. For a while they saw themselves as behavioural scientists who dealt with paintings instead of statistics. Oehlen was one of Polke's students, but he has been influenced by Beuys to a far greater extent.

Apart from painting, Oehlen also takes great interest in philosophy, and he has studied the works of Nietzsche quite intensively. One of his most significant paintings is called *The Appearance of Appearances* (1983). The painting is almost square, showing the contours of a woman on the right and a wheel and key on the left, against a background which is painted in a controlled but expressive manner. Sparsely placed coloured lines suggest space while at the same time negating it. The female figure is reminiscent of a naked dummy in a shop-window.

Georg Herold:
Beluga, 1989
Resin on canvas,
141 ⅝ × 82 ⅝ in.
(360 × 210 cm)
Galerie Max Hetzler, Cologne

The wheel has an element of sexual sadism about it. Title and painting cannot really be related to one another, although the title may be a description of Oehlen's artistic programme, his striking paintings of space, mirrors and mannequin dolls with their bewildering levels of perception. The appearance of appearances is the intensification of appearances, or rather their ironical duplication, which reduces their intensity. Thus the painting provides the opportunity to break the bogus appearance of art. What do these appearances hide? The filth of life. And when appearances are reduced to mere appearances, then one has reached the lowest layer of one's perceptive capacity, which – as the German literary scholar Karl Heinz Bohrer puts it – is the point of no return. In more concrete terms, one has reached the unimaginable, i.e. cruelty and filth. Nobody talks about it. It has been suppressed.

It is precisely this filth with which Büttner confronts the viewer in his scandalous painting *Self-Portrait, Masturbating in the Cinema* (1980). Far from betraying a smug kind of exhibitionism, which might aim at providing his dear public with a feast for the eye, it attacks us by dragging the relationship between artist and viewer down to the level of a peep show. Thus it exposes the rotten idea that the artist's ruthless display of his artistic ego could actually arouse more than a titillating desire for self-satisfaction in the viewer. Both Oehlen and Büttner are quite aware of the possibilities – or rather the impossibility – of today's art. The central theme of their art is aporia, i.e. a state of mind in which man pretends not to know what is going on. Nevertheless, Büttner, in particular, does not allow this insight to prevent him from exposing the contradictions that exist in our media-dominated society towards the turn of the millennium. The immediacy and the thickness of his painting style can therefore add quite a stunning effect at times.

Although Büttner and Oehlen, Kippenberger and Herold were not born in Berlin, they lived in the Western half of this divided city for quite a while – a place where the contradictions and antagonisms of post-war Western society are more tangible than anywhere else, more so even than in New York, the metropolis of capitalism and the art world. Nowhere in the world is there such a gulf between claim and reality, between reality and appearance, truth and lies. However, the truth always consists of a number of different perspectives. It is like a crystal in which the light is refracted into multitudes of different colours. Berlin, that city with an over-high percentage of the elderly, has also attracted many of the critically-minded intellectuals who have their roots in the student revolt of 1968. It is a refuge for German youngsters who want to avoid military service, a wide-open gate for asylum-seekers from all over the world, and the propagandist "shop window" of Western affluence and Western consumer society. Many Germans enjoy equating Berlin with unrestrained development of personal freedom, and it is therefore highly subsidized by the West German government to ensure the survival of the enclave which is surrounded by a "foreign" country – a country that used to be Berlin's own hinterland. In brief, Berlin is an artificial formation which even Hollywood could not have invented. From the artist's point of view, Berlin is a city without a traditional art collectors' culture, without trendy museums and without highly influential galleries. It is not so much a ghetto, as a cultural hothouse under a thick fog of provincialism, and this is the basis on which it has developed its own specific climate. Long-lost traditions, such as Expressionism and "Critical" Realism, survived in Berlin for much longer than anywhere else in West Germany. And whereas the latter has (so far) not had any significant effect on the art world, Expressionism could easily hibernate without its roots drying up.

Baselitz and Lüpertz started off in Berlin. Hödicke and – after a brief period of "exile" in Cologne – Koberling inspired an entire generation of artists with their Neo-Expressive art. It did, however, take quite a while before they found their own style, and it must be admitted

Werner Büttner:
Brothers with Music, 1984
Brüder mit Musik
Oil on canvas, 59 × 74¾ in.
(150 × 190 cm)
Private collection, Cologne

that the public was very slow to respond to this kind of art – even in Berlin. The lacklustre shabbiness of "Critical" Realism was still regarded as Berlin's trademark, while an insipid Constructivism was also (still) accepted, together with a general orientation towards typical avant-gardist trends. However, the tender plant of Neo-Expressionism was never choked to death, and it was probably inspiration from New York that made the artists take the matter into their own hands. They had always maintained close links with New York, and so they followed the example of their American colleagues and opened galleries in derelict factories in order to present their works to those who were interested. In other words, in Berlin the art that was proclaimed as "fierce" or "wild" was not initiated by any trend-setting institution.

It would certainly be wrong to claim that the explosion of young artistic talent in this city can be explained entirely in terms of the psychological pressure on Berlin artists. And yet there can be no doubt that something of this pressure is definitely present in the anger, the frantic activity and the immediacy of their paintings, especially the earlier ones. What is more, it was the massive number of outsiders, all flocking together in Berlin, who provided a highly charged cultural atmosphere – not within the official art scene, but outside it. Irving Penn, the famous fashion and still-life photographer, once described the climate in Manhattan as "electrifying", and to a lesser extent this is also true for Berlin. We can see, therefore, why Fetting, Middendorf and Bernd Zimmer had already been invited to give solo exhibitions at well-known New York galleries in the early eighties, before they began to gain ground in West Germany and the rest of Europe. However, there was a further reason: many of the New York galleries were owned by Jewish collectors, and these paintings from Berlin, which were bubbling over with forcefulness, meant that the Jewish gallery-owners could come face to face with their own past. After all, it was museum enthusiasts, collectors and traders of Jewish origin who had been instrumental in promoting "classical" German Expressionism. But what was equally important was the direct impact of these paintings – an impact which contributed significantly to their success in a city full of "hype" and pragmatism. Take, for instance, the abysmal loneliness in Fetting's pale and shady *Shower Paintings*, the shrill sound that virtually screams at you in Middendorf's *Musicians* series, or the hidden yearning for untouched nature in Zimmer's *Landscapes*.

Rainer Fetting is a highly gifted artist who has derived his inspiration above all from Francis Bacon and Van Gogh. The Dutch painter was so important to Fetting that he even wanted to act the part of Van Gogh in a film which he would have directed himself. Fetting's choice of subjects is determined by his own personal range of experiences. He would have loved to become a rock musician, and – like Middendorf, Salomé, Dahn and Markus Oehlen – he has played in rock groups from time to time. He paints in phases and then very rapidly, as if he deliberately intended to translate the ecstatic rhythm of rock music into visual images. His method of painting has been described as *performance*. Still, he never loosens his control over the actual process of painting, which is why his paintings appear to be cooler than Middendorf's. He always concentrates on a small number of subjects: portraits and self-portraits, city life and erotic scenes from the homosexual world. Whether Fetting looks at Berlin or New York – the two cities between which he commutes – it is never the glamorous world of the avenues and boulevards that is reflected in his paintings, but the world of outcasts in their pathetic housing estates by the Berlin Wall and the depressing New York subway stations. Fetting is a meticulous observer of such scenes, but he also takes sides. He acquired this spontaneous painting style during a visit in Salomé's studio, where he noticed that Salomé was full of tension when painting. He realized that he, too, had been making this mistake, and so he managed to help Salomé artistically, and also himself.

Salomé's paintings similarly plunge into an alien world, the glittering demi-monde of transvestites. While Fetting paints men in the same way that the artists of previous periods used to paint nude women, the creatures who populate Salomé's paintings are rather ambiguous in their sexuality. It is a world of dissolving contours, where nothing follows a familiar pattern, a world that propels the viewer into a confusion of conflicting feelings, like a rapid alternation of hot and cold showers. Salomé's *Swimmers* can be regarded as the most apt visual metaphor in this respect. What unites the paintings of the Berlin painters is not just a matter of themes and of subject matter; they portray an extraordinarily artificial world, so that there is always a certain theatrical effect in them. Although this is a world which really exists and not an imaginary one, the people in it move about as if they were on stage. These social outcasts, drop-outs, rockers, punks, homosexuals, transvestites and unemployed

Andreas Schulze:
Curtain, 1984
Vorhang
Dispersion on muslin, 90½ × 141¾ in.
(230 × 360 cm)
Galerie Monika Sprüth, Cologne

youngsters have all created their own world, with a strict code of behaviour. Thus the individual member is given an identity which would otherwise be in danger. And whenever they feel the pressure to conform to their environment, they radically overreact. Their stage-like existence, the pleasure of dressing up in a provocative way and of emphasizing their differences – these are all elements which have become second nature to them, as it were. It is the same zest which is expressed so vehemently in rock music, and rock musicians are therefore the most agile protagonists in Fetting and Middendorf's paintings. This artificiality is also seen in the settings of these works. In a way, it is as if the unreal world of black-and-white cinema screens had all of a sudden come to life, with characters like unpaid actors – fighting for survival.

Page 132:

Helmut Middendorf:
Aeroplane Dream, 1982
Flugzeugtraum
Synthetic resin on canvas,
157½ × 118⅛ in. (400 × 300 cm)
Galerie Gmyrek, Düsseldorf

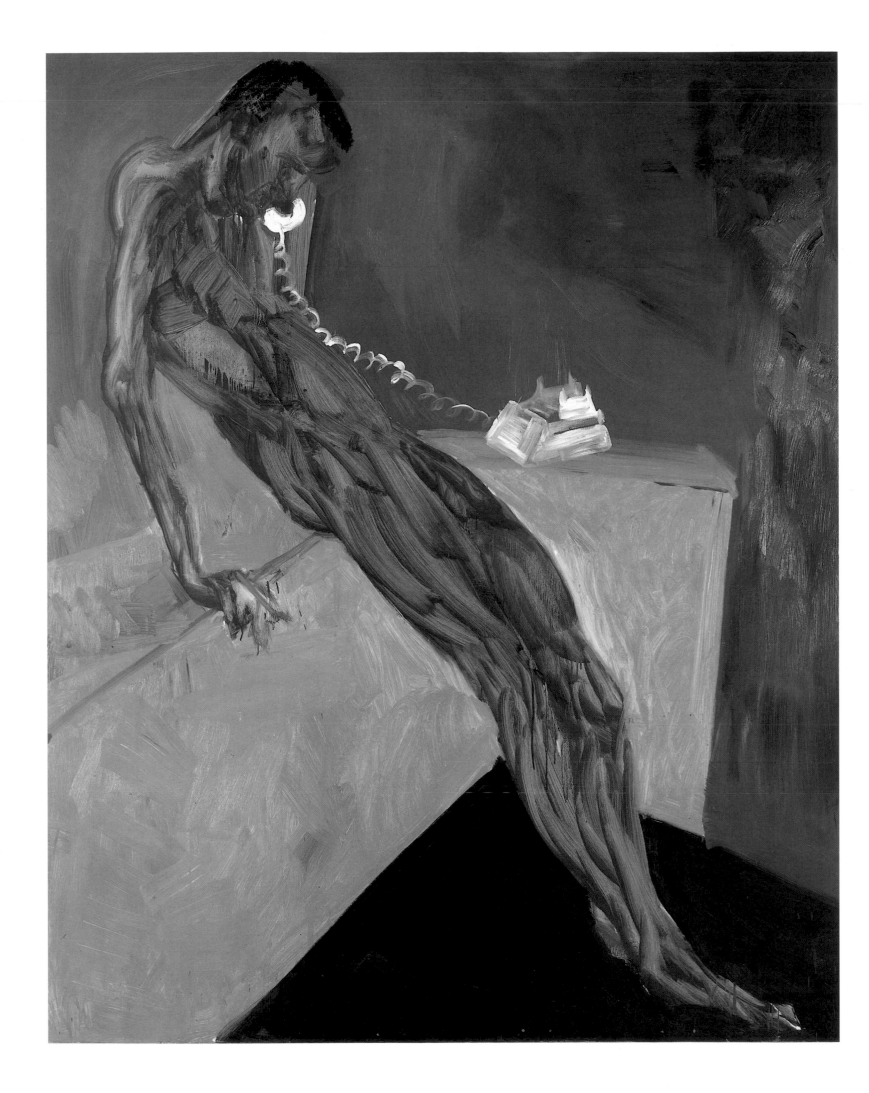

Bernd Zimmer:
Far – Near, 1985
Ferne – Nähe
Dispersion on canvas, 68⅞ × 88⅝ in.
(175 × 225 cm)
Karl Pfefferle Galerie & Edition, Munich

Page 134:

Rainer Fetting:
Phone Call, 1984
Acrylic on canvas, 90½ × 71⅝ in.
(230 × 182 cm)
Galerie Paul Maenz, Cologne

There is No Accounting for Taste

Hilton Kramer, an influential American art critic with conservative leanings, conceded that the return of representational tendencies in the world of art was quite a significant event. "It was pretty obvious: something important had happened. We were witnessing a real change of taste." Taste - this is a word which sounds odd to European ears. Kramer explains: "Taste somehow seems to obey the law of compensation, so that with the negation of certain qualities of a period one almost automatically prepares the ground for its triumphant return at a later stage, but it is never possible to predict exactly the schedule of taste. Its roots are in a deeper and more mysterious layer than mere fashion. I believe that what is at the core of every genuine change in taste is a biting sensation of loss, an existential pain – a feeling that something absolutely vital for the life of art has entered into a state of unbearable atrophy. And, at the deepest level, taste aims to provide an immediate remedy for this perceived lack." Oddly enough, however, this "change in taste" meant that an art form came into being which made up for a loss, but was in many ways *about* losses: the loss of emotions in a world of machines, the disappearance of one's identity at the expense of an unstable type of personality, and the alienation even towards one's own body. In their paintings the artists invoke these losses in exaggerated pictorial forms, and this may also explain why their art seems to be as noisy as punk music – shrill, bombastic and eye-splitting.

The New York art scene in particular has been brimming over with vitality during the last ten years. It is full of frenzy and frantic restlessness. In Lower Manhattan, north and south of Canal Street and also – later – in the dreaded Lower East Side, galleries have shot up everywhere. In places where, ten years ago, nobody would have dared to venture, noisy activity suddenly prevailed. At the same time, American art – at least from a European point of view – was experiencing an artistic collapse. However, this did not threaten the undisputed position of New York in the art market, a position which it had held since the decline of Paris at the end of the fifties. European artists were beginning to fill the gaps and challenging American self-confidence. The works of German artists in particular were having an unmistakable effect. Beuys, Richter, Polke, Immendorff and Baselitz even advanced to a position of models who were emulated by others. And the Italian artists Chia, Cucchi and Clemente were given almost as much attention. A large part of their success may of course have been based on the misconception that their works were more immediate than they really were. After all, Americans saw in this art the triumph of emotions and extreme subjectiveness, a demonstrative unfolding of colossal energies at the expense of reason, a layer of ironical brokenness which hides the depths of despair. Two painters, who rose to the heights of superstars of the American art world within a very short period and who planned this sudden rise very well, gave convincing evidence in their paintings that the response to post-avant-garde European art had been rather one-dimensional. At the same time, however, they also stand for a primaeval force in the artistic potential of American art and for its high flexibility. These two painters were Julian Schnabel and David Salle.

Schnabel's extroverted art combines heterogeneous and vastly different influences. These are mainly European, though they also include American Abstract Expressionism. He has incorporated impulses from art history, as well as the world of popular art and the mass media. Before achieving his breakthrough in New York he had spent some time in Europe,

"An artist can talk about one or two things he knows, and no more."
Enzo Cucchi, 1986

David Salle:
Dual Aspect Picture, 1986
Acrylic and oil on canvas, 156 × 117 in.
(396.2 × 297.2 cm)
Mary Boone Gallery, New York

David Salle:
Untitled, 1984
Watercolour on paper, 18 × 24 in.
(45.7 × 61 cm)
Mary Boone Gallery, New York

David Salle:
Untitled, 1984
Watercolour on paper, 25 × 79 in.
(63.5 × 78.7 cm)
Mary Boone Gallery, New York

David Salle:
Saltimbanques, 1986
Acrylic and oil on wood and canvas,
60 × 100 in. (152.4 × 254 cm)
Mary Boone Gallery, New York

taking a great deal of interest in Beuys's, Polke's and Kiefer's studios, picking up ideas, adapting and changing them. He then amalgamated these with ideas from other sources until the abundance of what he had soaked up resulted in that "primaeval material" (Schjedahl) which literally began to "spread" through all his paintings. Schnabel has an unerring instinct for the attractiveness of different surfaces and he savours them to the full in all possible variations. He paints on silk, animal hide and sackcloth, uses broken plates, antlers, parts of a car's bodywork, cotton wool, the insides of clocks and old pieces of wood. He quotes European myths and contemporary America. He seeks to overwhelm his public with gigantic paintings, and unfolds such an overpowering magic in his paintings that no special effect is too primitive for him as long as it serves the purpose of seducing the viewer. His intention, he says, is to captivate the public with his paintings. If it were not for the obvious emphasis on the artist's ego, one might in many ways feel reminded of Baroque art, especially in his preference for religious subjects. Occasionally, in fact, one cannot avoid the impression that he identifies with Sebastian, who died a martyr's death in a hail of arrows, or even the crucified Christ. The style he adopts is no less eclectic than his choice of materials. Figurative and abstract elements occur side by side, and symbols and metaphors seem to be employed at random. Somehow everything appears to be an enormous hotchpotch but is nonetheless fascinating. Nor does the artist seem to mind if people prefer certain parts of his paintings to others. It is as if Schnabel's pictorial orchestra were in complete disarray. Yet, there is a powerful suggestiveness in these cacophonies which draws us towards them without our noticing it.

Schnabel and Salle have been pursuing their artistic careers quite systematically. They are – to paraphrase the title of a film by Jean-Luc Godard – the children of Warhol and the NBC. They are stars of the U.S. art scene, and they feel like stars. They are not at all corrupted by the European idea of a genius. Schnabel's performances, in particular, are always mass spectacles. He receives the same kind of publicity as an American football star, and his spectacularly well-paid contract with the Pace Gallery in New York provoked the same headlines as Sylvester Stallone's fees. It goes without saying that Helmut Newton, the well-known society photographer, has photographed him and made him part of his portrait gallery of celebrities.

Page 141:

David Salle:
Making the Bed, 1985
Oil and acrylic on wood and canvas,
120 × 98 in. (304.8 × 248.9 cm)
Emily and Jerry Spiegel Collection,
New York

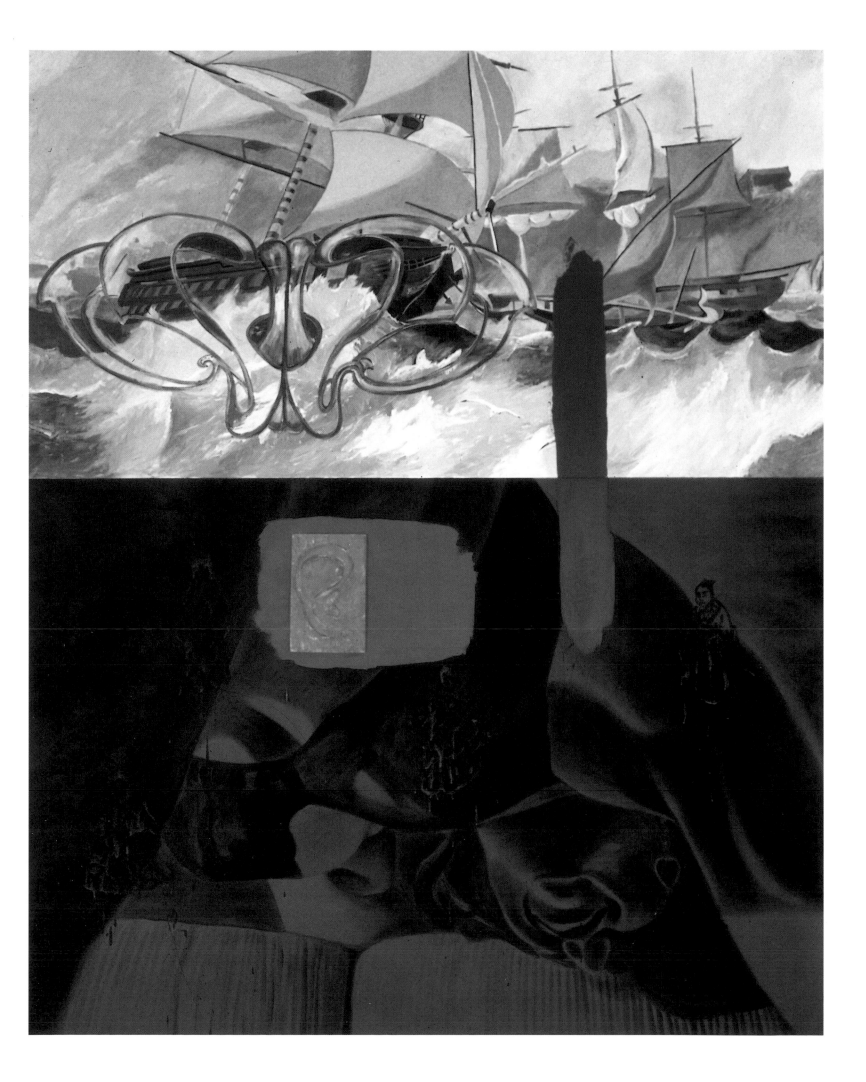

David Salle:
Muscular Paper, 1985
Oil on canvas, 98 × 187½ in.
(249 × 476 cm)
Mary Boone Gallery, New York

Eric Fischl:
Birthday Boy, 1983
Oil on canvas, 83⅞ × 108¼ in.
(213 × 275 cm)
Mary Boone Gallery, New York

David Salle gives the impression of being a little more aloof than Julian Schnabel, and he is said to be something of a cynic. However, he also has the reputation of being quite cunning and of refusing to let anybody steal his show. His career has been very similar to that of several German artists. Having received his training in the hey-day of Concept Art, he used to take a keen interest in video and the pictures of the mass media. A lot of these early interests can still be felt in his art today. His giant paintings occasionally combine to form diptychs and triptychs, and they are accompanied by intimate drawings which betray a more introverted temperament than his large, declamatory paintings. Salle, too, has an eclectic approach to art. His paintings contain both attractive and repulsive motifs from the widest possible range of available sources. He uses pornographic magazines as well as highly meaningful but encoded paintings from serious art, both from popular introductions to drawing and painting and from awe-inspiring historical tomes. Salle combines these motifs in an integral whole that is full of tension and never dissolves in pleasant harmonies. He projects the various subjects on top of one another, e.g. the contours of an enticing nude against the diffused background of a colour-field painting. His paintings are a symptomatic illustration of the bewildering visual repertoire of modern man and modern civilization.

Salle's artistic method is parallelled in the work of the German painter Stefan Szczesny, who also combines the subjects of a wide variety of different times and inventories. Salle, however, is more rigorous and extreme in his choice, more daring in what he combines. It was from Polke that he learnt the technique of transparent painting: the painter paints subjects of totally different origins, one on top of the other. These layers yield irritating spatial formations in which the subject of the painting itself clashes in an odd kind of way with the transparent surface, so that there is no unity whatsoever. Polke had copied this technique from Francis Picabia's works of the thirties, and Salle has obviously mastered it completely. Superimposed upon the human contours of his male and female nudes, often in provocative postures, Salle's heterogeneous paintings are both in an abstract vein and include naturalist photo-painting techniques, with the occasional hint of the social realism that prevailed during the American Depression. The structure of his paintings is extremely complex – a reflection, as it were, of the complex appearances of our world, where ideas and mental images, once they have become visual, are considered to be just as real as the phenomena which are physically tangible or can be experienced psychologically.

At the 1985 Paris Biennial Exhibition paintings by the American artist Eric Fischl hung beside paintings by Kiefer. This challenging contrast was highly illuminating and, at the same time, somewhat questionable. The differences between the two became as obvious as their common points. Fischl gives the observer some insight into the inner workings of North American life, whereas Kiefer sheds some light on the hidden recesses of the German mind. At first sight Fischl appears to be a realistic painter, though not in the ordinary sense of the word. His paintings are filled with a strong element of sexual obsession, which is also reflected in the powerful directness of his subjects. And yet the light in which they are submerged makes them radiate a strange intensity. One does not get the impression that they have been transposed from one reality into another, i.e. from the world of everyday life to the sphere of art, but rather that they are modern mythical images. And so it is not surprising that their vibrant sexuality reveals the fundamental psychological causes of numerous social neuroses, which are particularly widespread in the U.S. Although many of his subjects seem to be the artistic expression of his own childhood traumas, Fischl constructs the events in his paintings from ideas which are expressed in his own photographs and those of other people.

Eric Fischl:
Bad Boy, 1981
Oil on canvas, 66⅛ x 96 in.
(168 × 244 cm)
Mary Boone Gallery, New York

Eric Fischl:
Sleepwalker, 1979
Oil on canvas, 72 × 108 (183 × 274 cm)
Mary Boone Gallery, New York

Page 147:

Eric Fischl:
Best Western, 1983
Oil on canvas, 108 × 77½ in.
(274 × 197 cm)
Mary Boone Gallery, New York

Eric Fischl:
Cargo Cults, 1984
Oil on canvas, 90½ × 132 in.
(230 × 335 cm)
Mary Boone Gallery, New York

This wave of inspiration merges the spheres of privacy with the more public domain, and it also shows that Fischl does not depict the material world of everyday experience, but rather the dream world of desires and anxieties. His colours are generally off, and his canvases are dominated by a dirty-grey ochre or a brownish ochre or a dark blue, mingled with a sombre grey-green which has recently started to turn into a brighter bottle-like green. But it is always Fischl's special use of light that gives the scenes their unforgettable aura. There is a blatant ugliness about the way the paint has been applied, a rather nonchalant treatment of shapes and colours, in keeping with the character of the subject matter, which would otherwise degenerate into a sticky kind of naturalism. In this way the painter reduces the voyeurist aspect of his paintings. Such a perspective is undoubtedly always present, of course, and in view of the scenes which Fischl reveals, the viewer cannot help feeling that he is involuntarily witnessing something very intimate. However, instead of sneaking away quietly, he is absolutely spellbound and continues to look at it with fascination. One assimilates the artist's lewd perspective and discovers that one is in fact just as lewd. Perceiving, observing, taking a good look at something - surely these activities of the human eye and mind are really rather indecent, inquisitive and perhaps even perverse? This is certainly true for Fischl's paintings. In fact, Donald Kuspit maintains that there is a general element of perversion in American realism and the various artistic currents descended from it. "This realism functions wherever there is a desire for immediate perception as a breach of expectations, and it therefore has a morbidly fascinating effect, laying claim to the beholder on a voyeurist level and educating him in a fetishistic sense. In my theory, perception is a perverse activity with a perverse object – reality; but perversity is not explained, only implied, it is not made explicit, only insinuated."

Fischl's perspective is usually that of a little boy or a stranger, thus giving his paintings an urgency which stuns or even horrifies the viewer. Unlike in his earlier paintings, Fischl can now force a voyeurist perspective on the public without using a figure with whom one might be able to identify. His paintings show the American middle classes in the most private and intimate situations, and we can feel the sexual tension that permeates the languid sluggishness of their leisure activities. The people in the paintings lurk and skulk while at the same time being totally perplexed, and we can see hidden anxieties flickering in their eyes: there is a boy staring at the genitalia of a masturbating woman while stealing something from her; a girl overtly offering herself to a boy who is sexually aroused; a girl switching channels on the television set while copulating with a man; and a woman watching another woman drying her genitals. The protagonist's perspective in Fischl's paintings intersects with that of the beholder, and it is the latter who feels that he has been caught in the act. However, rather than turning away, he is fascinated – and at the same time unsettled – thus becoming an accomplice. Like other artists, Fischl sets the stage in each painting as if it were a dramatic theatre play, with heavy shadows and plenty of contrast, as in Philip Pearlstein's films, with lighting effects that are more typical of the film studio. The world has become a stage where people act their roles with an attitude of excessive self-love and exhibitionism, not cheerfully but as if there were nothing they could do to forestall the impending disaster. It seems as though Shakespeare's sombre visions are casting their shadows on Fischl's paintings.

Robert Longo has created a monster that might have come from a *Star Wars* film by George Lucas – a creature that expresses the artist's horror visions and forebodings, a mixture of "Boccioni and Hollywood." (Edward F. Fry) Longo is a typical representative of the post-avant-garde art. He has no inhibitions about the aesthetic material he employs and he is totally nonchalant about films and T.V. He sees himself not only as an artist who produces paintings, drawings and sculptures, but also as a musician and actor, as a film producer and as a graphic designer. He is not afraid of competition from the mass media or of losing his public to them. "My aim is to make art which can hold its own against television, films and magazines." Longo's artistic subjects are power and violence – the violence of wars and the power of the corporations that unleash them. Power and violence make people reel with giddiness, and in Longo's installations and paintings they dance and reel in uncontrolled contortions. It is often impossible to tell what has prompted these ecstatic movements – whether it was the frenzied sound of music or the deadly wartime bullet. There are no clear distinctions between the violence of a war, the violence of everyday life and the violence in the mass media. Longo has re-introduced an attitude to the world of art which also prevailed among artists during the time of Baroque. Unlike Baroque artists, of course, he does not

Jean-Michel Basquiat:
Cadillac Moon, 1981
Acrylic and crayon on canvas,
63 × 68 in. (162.5 × 172.7 cm)
Sammlung Bruno Bischofberger, Zurich
Küsnacht

Jean-Michel Basquiat:
Max Roach, 1984
Acrylic on canvas, 60 × 60 in.
(152.5 × 152.5 cm)
Sammlung Bruno Bischofberger, Zurich
Küsnacht

Page 153:

Jean-Michel Basquiat:
Tobacco (Tabac), 1984
Acrylic and oil crayon on canvas,
86¼ × 68⅛ in. (219 × 173 cm)
Sammlung Bruno Bischofberger, Zurich
Küsnacht

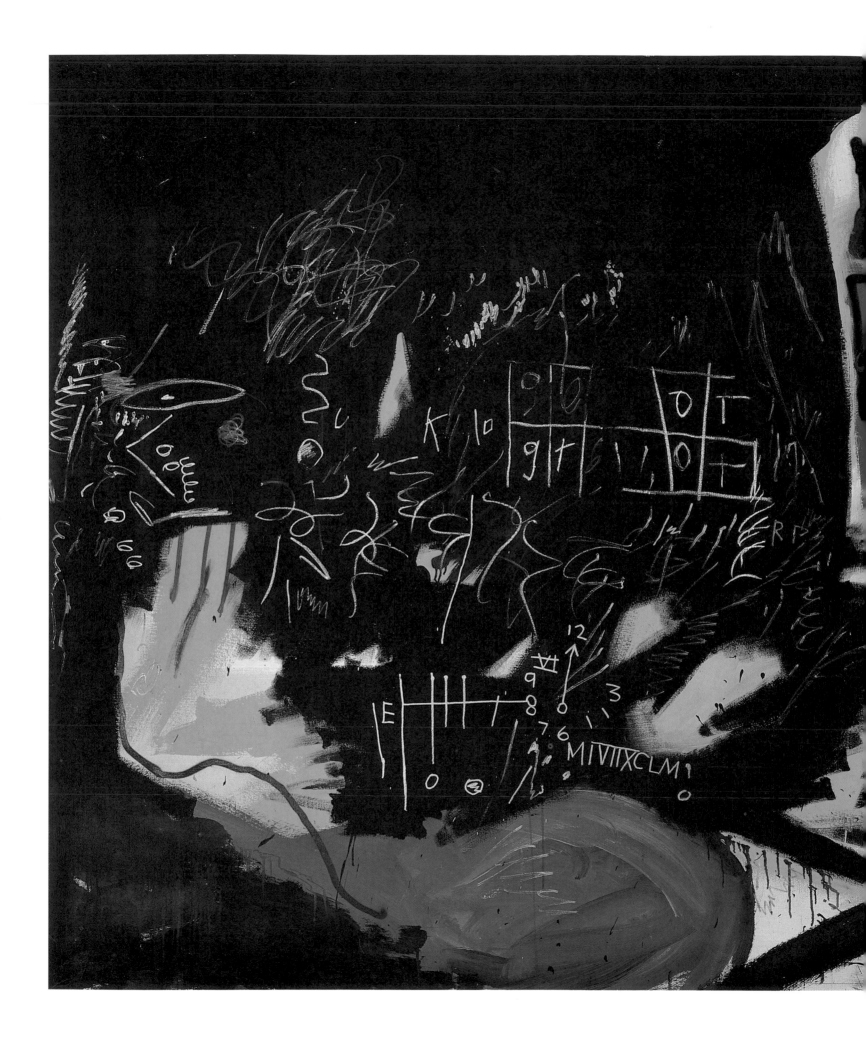

Pages 154/155:

Jean-Michel Basquiat:
Profit I, 1982
Acrylic and oil on canvas,
86⅝ × 157½ in. (220 × 400 cm)
Sammlung Bruno Bischofberger, Zurich
Küsnacht

Julian Schnabel:
The Student of Prague, 1983
Oil, plate and gelatine on wood,
116 × 228 in. (294.6 × 579.1 cm)
Emily and Jerry Spiegel Collection,
New York

usually take on commissioned work, and his art is based entirely on his own ideas. However, like them, he sees himself as making full use of artistic means and opportunities and concentrates first and foremost on the effect. It was the world of the theatre which inspired him, with its entire apparatus for arousing feelings and passions, and his love of the stage is particularly reflected in his installations. There is no shortage of special effects in his art, which seeks to drown the shrill noise of the mass media with visual stimuli that are even more strident. Unlike Fischl, Longo does not dissect the human soul, though he is a deeply committed artist. Like Schnabel, he endeavours to overwhelm the viewer with a tremendous barrage of material and means of representation. He wants to drive out the devil by Beelzebub, as it were, and one feels inclined to wonder if perhaps the quiet subversiveness of Salle and Fischl might not ultimately yield more tangible insights than Longo's thunderously theatrical emphasis on the spectacular.

Before a new form of art that was both representational and expressive could gain recognition in the U.S., the American art world had to undergo a lengthy developmental process often concealed from the European eye. Although Minimal and Concept Art dominated the museums and the more enlightened galleries, this delay is all the more difficult to understand if one considers that American collectors, who are far more influential in the art world than their European counterparts, were considerably more cautious, and the purist tendencies in the art world had had practically no effect on the way Americans chose to see themselves. It was artists like Philip Guston, Malcolm Morely, Neil Jenny and Susan Rothenberg, as well as Pattern & Decoration and the various popular street cultures that paved the way for figurative, expressive movements and brought about the "change in taste" which the art critic Kramer spoke of, a change which was fully in keeping with American artistic traditions. Also, we must not forget someone as active, inventive and intelligent as Gordon Matta-Clark who, incidentally, far surpassed the work of nearly all his contemporaries. He was the artist who realized at a very early stage that the garishly painted New York subway trains were in fact artistic statements that should be taken very seriously. He displayed photographs of these rattling monsters in exhibitions outside the established art market. This indefatigable promoter of an artistic revolution, who died at the early age of 33, had seen how much creative imagination as well as cultural and political explosiveness was beginning to

Julian Schnabel:
The Sea, 1981
Mexican potsherds, plaster and oil on canvas
108 × 156 in. (274.3 × 396.3 cm)

unfold both in and around these subway trains. To European eyes it seemed like a refreshing break from the artistic sterility of Minimal Art, whereas people who worked in the skyscrapers of Midtown Manhattan thought it was rather an eyesore. And so the artist, Jean-Michel Basquiat, had already become quite famous – or rather infamous – in New York, a long time before his real name had made the rounds in the art world of the city. Basquiat was Samo. His cryptograms, crowns and copyright signs had already been seen, or at least unconsciously registered, by everyone in New York. Samo was the New York graffiti writer and artist *par excellence*. In the relevant circles he was generally accepted as their "king". He had worked his way to the top of that pyramid, a hierarchically structured model of society, which had moulded the graffiti culture just as it had shaped the structure of society as a whole.

Basquiat, whose mother came from Puerto Rico and his father from Haiti, was born in Brooklyn, which has since become one of the most infamous parts of New York. His parents divorced, he changed schools frequently and even spent a few months in Puerto Rico – all in all, conditions which were far from ideal for the career of an American artist. His artistic ambitions were initially aimed at becoming a cartoonist, and the topics he preferred were Hitchcock, Nixon, cars, war, weapons, and the legendary and controversial FBI chief, J. Edgar Hoover. Unlike his artistic contemporary Keith Haring, who was at times the object of great admiration and applause in the New York art world, Basquiat did not enter the realm of

Page 158:

Julian Schnabel:
The Return from the Hospital, 1982
Oil on wood, 122 × 71 in.
(309.9 × 180.3 cm)
Emily and Jerry Spiegel Collection,
New York

Julian Schnabel:
The Dancers (for Pasolini), 1977/78
Oil on canvas, 72 × 84 in.
(182.9 × 213.4 cm)
Emily and Jerry Spiegel Collection,
New York

promoted art through traditional artistic training, but came to it from outside. He is an artist who embodies the second revolution of the American art world, following an earlier breakthrough at the end of the seventies when, for the first time, women were completely accepted as artists. Basquiat represents one of those classes in American society that are normally barred from artistic careers (with the exception of music and, more recently, also literature). These are the black and Hispanic minorities. His paintings, painted objects and drawings are full of signs, texts and figurative elements which add up to breathtakingly confident rhythmic patterns – a mixture of scriptural paintings, popular American symbolism, street jargon and allusions to famous works from art history. What is truly amazing is the peculiar affinity of his art to that of Jean Dubuffet, Cy Twombly and A.R. Penck. This may or may not be coincidence, but if one ignores his rather important references to the social position of America's coloured population and the considerable anger expressed in his paintings, one might in fact conclude that Basquiat's paintings and drawings are rooted in French aesthetics, rather than in New York's graffiti culture.

Quite a lot has been written about graffiti artists, and some of their work has been over-estimated and enthusiastically overrated. But as soon as the commercial art market ravenously began to claim these artists, their aggressiveness was broken, and their total disregard for convention, which had on occasion assumed outrageous proportions, was replaced by thin-blooded routine. Basquiat knew how to protect himself against such a downfall, and the Swiss Bischofsberger Gallery, which acted as his representative, handled his exhibition schedule very sensibly, so that his interests were fully protected. In November 1982 Basquiat had his first important exhibition at the Fun Gallery in the middle of Manhattan's Lower East Side – the sort of area which one would not normally wish to enter without a bodyguard. The gallery owes its name to Kenny Scharf, who is also a graffiti artist. One of the gallery's most

Robert Longo:
Now Everybody 1982/83
Mixed media, 96 × 192 in. (243.9 × 487.7 cm)
and 79 × 28 × 115 in.
(200.7 × 71.1 × 114.3 cm)
Neue Galerie, Ludwig Collection, Aachen

Robert Longo:
Corporate Wars: Wall of Influence, 1982
Middle portion, aluminium cast,
83⅞ × 107⅞ in. (213 × 274 cm)
Saatchi Collection, London

Two friends ran into each other at the door of a psychiatrist's office.
"Are you coming or going?" asked one. The other replied, "If I knew, I wouldn't be here."

Peter Halley:
Black Cell with Conduit Twice, 1988
day-glo acryl, roll-a-tex on canvas,
64 × 128 in. (162.5 × 325 cm)
Galerie Jablonka, Cologne

Page 162:

Richard Prince:
Coming or Going, 1988
Acrylic and silkscreen on canvas,
55 ⅞ × 48 in. (142 × 122 cm)
Jablonka Galerie, Cologne

enterprising directors was Patty Astor, who had acted the role of a critic in Charlie Ahearn's *Wild Style*. This was an impressive film on the graffiti scene in which the protagonist, the graffiti artist Lee Quinones, simply acted himself. The film calls to mind the social and cultural conditions which triggered off this undercurrent of artistic protest, and it also touches upon the heated discussion that went on among graffiti artists and finally culminated in a breach between those who became integrated in the art scene and those who rejected such a development. A number of gifted artists have survived, above all Basquiat, but also Scharf, David Wojnarowicz, Rhonda Zwillinger, and Haring, who is more at home in American Pop Art and has continued its tradition into the eighties. What has also remained is the discovery of the vibrant artistic cosmos of the street, a discovery which is now taken for granted; in fact, for the art dealer Tony Shafrazi graffiti is "the most exciting art" that has ever existed.

Next to Basquiat, the most original of these graffiti artists is Scharf. In his brightly colourful paintings he creates a cheerful hotchpotch of Renaissance art, Surrealism and objects from the world of comics and the mass media. Like his friend Haring, he is not really an authentic graffiti artist, but someone who learnt his trade at an art college. However, although his art and that of his colleagues is highly original, it raises the legitimate question whether one can really get away with trying to outdo the visual stimuli of the photographic and electronic media by means of even more garish optical stimuli.

Admittedly, our first impression is that these works of art are "mind-blowing", that they "turn you on", or whatever other fashionable phrases one may wish to use. But what is also true is that such effects can quite easily neutralize each other, that they can blunt our perception instead of sharpening it. In fact, after only a short while, most of these artistic graffiti creations effectively ring just as hollow as the visual rubbish of commercial mass culture.

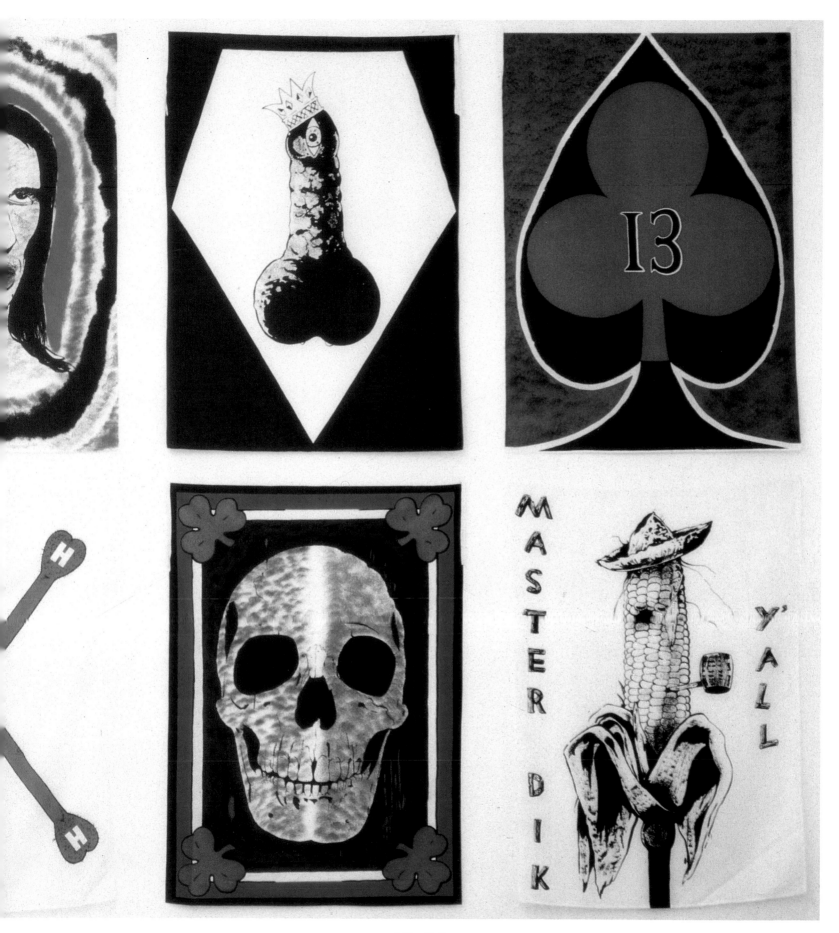

Mike Kelley:
Pansy Metal Covered Hoof, 1989
10 oversized silk
scarvers, edition of 40,
52 ⅞ × 38 in.
Galerie Gisela Capitain

Staging Reality or the Power of Photography

As Jürgen Klauke says of himself, he uses a camera where other artists use a paintbrush or a pencil. Jürgen Klauke is a German painter, drawer, performance artist and photographer. However, he does not really use a camera at all, but employs a photographer who then records his artistic ideas. Klauke designs and arranges what he wants the camera to record. And recently he has begun to subject his photographic material to further artistic processing, once it has left the laboratory. Photography is a medium which artists have always found rather problematic. One tends to forget that about 150 years ago it was hailed with great enthusiasm by a number of artists and critics who agreed with the academic painter Paul Delaroche and maintained that the art of painting was now finally dead. Another fact which has long been suppressed is that numerous artists, who were actually quite sceptical about photography, wholeheartedly welcomed it as a source for motifs and subjects. Yet photography is still fighting for its artistic legitimacy. When an influential book on photography by Pierre Bourdieu was translated into German, it was published under the apt title *Eine illegitime Kunst* ("An Illegitimate Art"), which was undoubtedly justified. During the 1920s there was a short period when photography was extremely popular as an artistic medium, i.e. in Russian avant-garde and progressive *Bauhaus* art. Man Ray, on the other hand, whose name has gone down in the history of both art and photography, thought of himself mainly as an artist and regarded photography as a bread-and-butter job. Yet his photographs, including the ones on fashion, were artistically superior to his paintings.

It was not until Concept Art that artists began to take an interest in photography again. After all, together with the spoken and the printed language, it was a vehicle which carried artistic notions and ideas. When photography made its re-entry into the world of art, it did so with relatively modest paintings and without any clever artistic devices. Confronted with a reality that was becoming more and more distorted by images of a mechanical and electronic kind, it somehow fulfilled its intended purpose because it was so unpretentious and spontaneous. Since then artists have been developing a far more self-confident attitude towards the different possibilities of photography. Again, Polke was one of the artists who had paved the way for this change in attitudes. Not even the powerful revival of the art of painting in the eighties could reduce the surge of interest in photography as an artistic medium of expression.

It is the power of technologically produced pictures over the human mind and human behaviour which is at the centre of Cindy Sherman's photo-pieces. These works are an excellent reflection of the omnipresent world of the commercial media. She is a photographer, actress, film director, scriptwriter, stylist, make-up assistant, hairdresser, stage designer and lighting specialist – a complete film team all rolled into one. And although her artistic tool has always been photography, the rhetoric of her art is clearly that of the film. One might say that Cindy Sherman projects a whole film into a single photo-piece, a film with only one actress – herself. This does not mean, however, that her pictures are full of vanity and self-admiration. Again and again, the actress assumes different parts - roles that are actively promoted by films and magazines, and above all by society, which imposes certain behavioural patterns on people, and especially on women. Most of these have ossified into clichés. What makes Cindy Sherman such a Protean actress is the way in which she adapts these roles, while at the same time breaking their tendency to become conventional. She does

Günther Förg:
Lingotte III, 1989
Colour photograph, framed,
106 ¼ × 70 ⅞ in.
(270 × 180 cm)
Galerie Max Hetzler, Cologne

167

so by constantly altering them, while her own ego remains completely concealed. Instead, her pictures tell whole stories about the yearnings, wishes and dreams, but also the secret anxieties and dangers that most women in our Western consumer society face. Cindy Sherman creates roles and images which already exist, and it is mainly films which provide her with plenty of material, though on one occasion her ideas came from a well-known sex magazine. Commissioned by an art magazine, she took a series of photographs modelled on the aesthetics and scenarios of the centrefolds of popular sex magazines. However, the publisher decided not to print this series after all. Was he perhaps afraid to frustrate people's secret macho longings?

During an important stage in the development of Cindy Sherman's art she concentrated on the social determination of the individual. This phase was accompanied by a change of style in the arrangement of her settings. In her previous works, where she had "quoted" from films, she used to create large pictorial spaces, richly furnished with props, so that the actual models somehow got lost in them. Now, however, the model became the dominating subject in her melodramatic photographs. The artist's camera began to focus more closely on the actual model, capturing her in such a way that the frame became like a cage. A young woman, idly lying on a couch and staring at a telephone, which has been ostentatiously placed in the foreground, seems literally "caged in" by the picture frame. On the other hand, one feels the suggestive force of her icon-like imagery gradually increase before the mind's eye and surround the model with an atmosphere of paralyzing iciness. Gone is the playfulness of black-and-white photos and also the charmingly nostalgic aura of her "film quotes". It is the element of criticism which has now come to the fore. The American critic Carter Ratcliffe concludes that the women she photographs – i.e. the advertising model, the trained little kitten, the fashion model and the sex object – are totally limited in their choice, with only a very limited number of options available to them. However, the artist did not confine herself to the critical depiction of negative ideas. Set against the cliché images and stereotyped roles that confront women in the West, she created pictures of a more rebellious type of woman: the pirate, the witch and the gypsy now took the place of "the nice girl next door". Fairy-tale

Jürgen Klauke:
Home Game, 1985
Heimspiel
Mixed media on paper, 59 × 94½ in.
(150 × 240 cm)

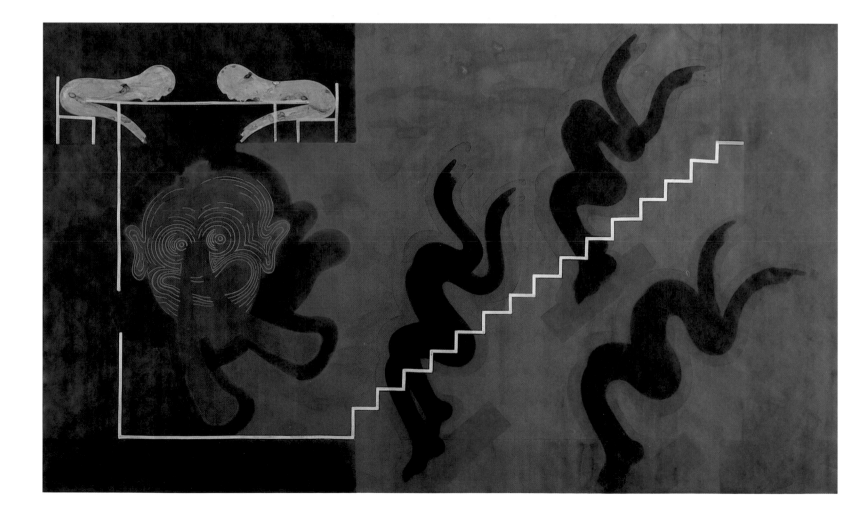

creatures began to emerge, such as a harem inmate with artificial breasts strapped to her, a demon-like being with a pig's snout. There is a subliminal aggressiveness which emanates from these pictures, a certain rebellion against stereotyped ideals of beauty. "I want that choked-up feeling in your throat," says Cindy Sherman, "which maybe comes from despair or teary-eyed sentimentality: conveying intangible emotions."

Astrid Klein:
Cerebral Somersault, 1984
Großhirnsalto
Photo-piece, 96½ × 50 in.
(245 × 127 cm)

Before Cindy Sherman it was Klauke who had reacted to the stereotyped roles within society. But whereas Cindy Sherman develops her artistic ideas on the basis of the existing world, with all its images and social fixations, Klauke was fascinated by the actual role patterns before they were reproduced and thus confirmed. The object of his art is not the world of reprographics, but ordinary human behaviour as found in the real world. This, too, is subject to conventions, constraints and norms, and Klauke is an artist who often puts his finger on those areas where conventions and norms can be revealed as empty rituals, where society has ceased to justify them and where they have degenerated into mere formulas which restrict a person's psychological development.

Klauke has devoted numerous performances and photographic series to his most important subject – sex. But the pictures he has created – whether on stage or as photographs – are totally different from commercial photographs on this subject. The expectations aroused by the latter are dashed in Klauke's work, which is intended to give the viewer food for thought, and it achieves this objective by showing him the gulf which separates desires from reality. At the same time, it also speaks about the desires and longings resulting from the constraints of fixed role allocations in society. Why should men look masculine and women feminine?

Under the heading *Masculine/Feminine* Klauke has produced several series of photos on sexual role distribution in society. He himself acted the part of an effeminate man, wearing feminine attributes and women's accessories. And yet these photographs are just as remote from transvestism as Katharina Sieverding's masculine self-portraits – photographs which were taken at the same time. Rather, Katharina Sieverding and Klauke wanted to express their disapproval of the stereotype role images of men and women in our Western society – an image with social and psychological consequences, and one that is certainly not limited to the aesthetic dimension.

In the mid-seventies Klauke extended his repertoire and ceased to take an almost exclusive interest in his own person. He created a number of wide-ranging photographic series in which he presented some extremely basic patterns of interpersonal behaviour, so basic in fact that

169

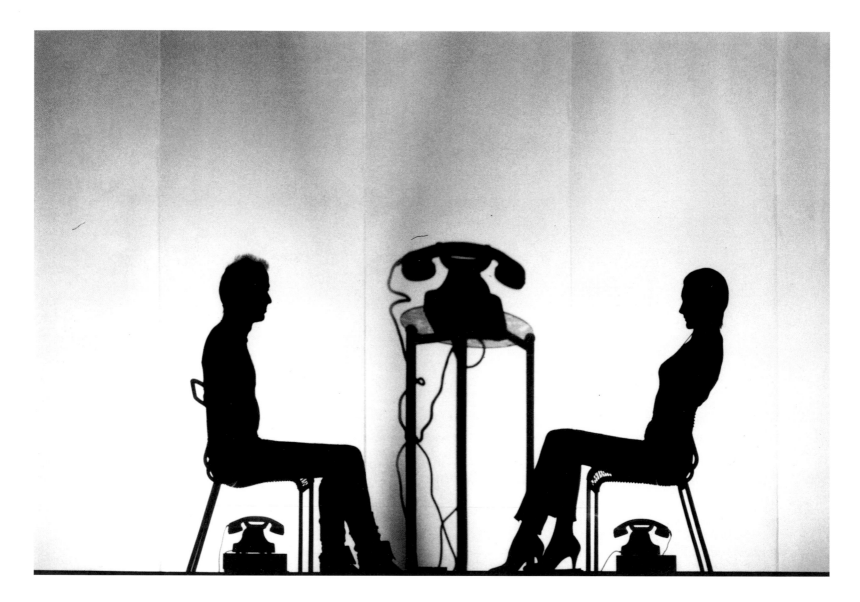

Jürgen Klauke:
From: Shadow Pictures, 1984
Schattenbilder
Photo-piece, 49¼ × 72⅞ in.
(125 × 185 cm)

Cindy Sherman:
Untitled, 1985
Colour photograph, both 72⅓ × 49⅓ in.
(184.2 × 125 cm)

they seemed more like models. Each scene was staged in such a way that only two, sometimes three, actors could be accommodated, thus reducing the general ambience to a state of complete sparseness. The choice of colour was strictly limited to black and white. The complete spectrum of human existence developed entirely from the actions of the characters, actions which were marked by ritualized precision. Their overall effect, however, could only become visible and be experienced by means of negation, i.e. by indicating a loss – loneliness and speechlessness, sometimes under a layer of fierce aggression, an autistic fear of being touched, indifference and boredom, shot through with subliminal erotic tension. These are the conspicuous themes of Klauke's art. Such topics are generally avoided by glossy magazines and advertising, and are not normally shown on television until the small hours of the morning. Klauke, who usually prepares his photographic work with numerous sketches, tries to break the power of technologically produced images by means of subversive artistic techniques, thus filling the gaps which have been left by the commercial pictures. "There are enough photographs," he says, "and most of them are quite superfluous, which is why mine could be called anti-photos - pictures that go against the tide of those reproductions which pretend to be about real life." Using the medium of photography, the artist penetrates the reality he has photographed and sheds some light on the illusions they create.

Another German artist who endeavours to debunk the supposed realism of photographed scenes is Bernhard Johannes Blume. Like Klauke, Katharina Sieverding, Urs Lüthi, Milan Kunc, Günther Förg, Christian Boltanski, Astrid Klein and of course Sigmar Polke, he never received any training as a photographer. He did, however, gain some experience when, as a child, he used to watch his mother develop masses of photographs. Blume, who is excellent at drawing and whose drawings gave an important impetus to Neo-Figurative art in Germany, concentrates in his photographs on what appears to be normal, everyday life. He shows extracts from everyday life and distorts them to the point where they become sequences of grotesque horrors, fluctuating between extreme hilarity and sheer panic, pictures that trigger off a feeling of irritated amusement in the viewer. If it were not for the element of travesty, which often triumphs over the horror in his pictures, one might think that quite a few of them had been inspired by Alfred Hitchcock. Blume has completely abandoned any claim that his pictures might have a documentary function. China or ceramic vases go into convulsions as if they were made of plasticine, vegetables suddenly refuse to be eaten, and simple everyday objects start flying about as if the law of gravity had been suspended. His wife, Anna Blume sometimes acts as a protagonist in his photographic stories about everyday life and sometimes

Bottom left:

Rob Scholte:
The Scream, 1985
De Schreeuw
Acrylic on canvas, 78¾ × 78¾ in.
(200 × 200 cm)
Galerie Paul Maenz, Cologne

Bottom right:

Rob Scholte:
Two Lesbians Mocking, 1983
Bespotting door twee potten
Acrylic on muslin, 59 × 59 in.
(150 × 150 cm)
Galerie Paul Maenz, Cologne

gives him new ideas or acts as an assistant. Together they conjure up an artistic universe that only exists as scenarios or mental images by using a medium which actually has a reputation for creating authentic images. The world has become like a film, and the viewer cannot help being amazed at this "reality", which is really no more than the product of his imagination. Again, Anna and Bernhard Blume's images must be seen as counter-images, directed against reality as it is normally photographed and against the illusions which are deliberately created.

One might ask if, at the end of the 20th century, the pictures of the cinema, television, magazines and advertisements in the West actually have more power over the human mind than one might be prepared to admit openly. There was certainly a grain of truth to it when a well-known German advertising specialist declared that advertisers were the real post-avant-garde artists, because they were the only ones who actually reached the public. It is to the credit of post-avant-garde artists that they have taken up this challenge. Even when it became obvious that aesthetic innovations can generally be dulled and exploited commercially, they were not deterred from continuing with their art. Confronted with the false glamour and deceptive realism of commercially produced images, the artists have countered these with photographic and videographic images that cast considerable doubt on the false beauty of their commercial counterparts. By skilfully manipulating their material, the artists have either exaggerated the appearance of beauty until it becomes totally improbable (as do Blume, the Dutch artists Henk Tas and Teun Hocks and the American multi-media virtuoso William Wegman), or they have shattered it by frivolously combining glossy aestheticism with

Henk Tas:
Holy Cow II, 1986
Photograph, mixed media,
23⅝ × 31½ in. (60 × 80 cm)
Torch, Amsterdam

Page 174:

William Wegman:
Snap and Chanel, 1982
Polaroid photograph, 24 × 20 in.
(61 × 51 cm)
Holly Solomon Gallery, New York

Page 175:

Cindy Sherman:
Untitled, 1983
Colour photograph, 72½ × 49¼ in.
(184.2 × 125 cm)

Bernhard Johannes and Anna Blume:
Kitchen Tantrums, 1986/87
Küchenkoller
Photo-piece, 51⅛ × 35⅞ in. (130 × 91 cm) and
78¾ × 51⅛ in. (200 × 130 cm)

Katharina Sieverding:
Continental Nucleus III/XXVI, 1986
Kontinentalkern III/XXVI
Photo-piece, 163¾ × 186¼ in.
(416 × 473 cm)

Page 178:

Thomas Ruff:
„Stars" 01 h 55–30°, 1990
„Sterne" 01 h 55–30°
C-print on plexi,
99 ¼ × 70 ⅞ in.
(252 × 180 cm)
Galerie Jonen & Schöttle, Cologne

Page 179:

Milan Kunc:
The World is Unfathomable, 1986
Die Welt ist unauslotbar
Oil on canvas, 47¼ × 37⅜ in.
(120 × 95 cm)
Galerie Monika Sprüth, Cologne

Barbara Kruger:
Installation April – June 1987
Galerie Monika Sprüth, Cologne

an atmosphere of doom and disaster (as in the works of Katharina Sieverding and Astrid Klein). The technologically produced pictures of the artists are in no way inferior to professional advertisements – neither in quality nor size – and their artistic inventiveness usually puts the commercial ones to shame. Their methods are more subtle, and their artistic universe goes far beyond the confines of photographic naturalism. Using the available flood of visual images, they have constructed a world which is doubly artificial.

Katharina Sieverding, for instance, photographed a four-engine World War II bomber straight from the television screen and then enlarged it out of all proportion, thus achieving a multiple alienation which turned the picture into a repulsive symbol of obscene violence. Astrid Klein's large-format photographs, populated by the shadowy contours of people, animals and buildings, have an uncanny immediacy about them, which only unfolds after lengthy, complicated darkroom work. We are inundated daily by a flood of visual impressions so numerous that we can no longer take them in. Katharina Sieverding and Astrid Klein, however, have developed their own way of choosing pictures from among this never-ending flood. And so they have succeeded in showing flashes of genuine reality and redeeming the messages of mass media pictures, which have become devoid of meaning. Seen superficially, the two artists hardly proceed any differently from advertising specialists in London, New York, Frankfurt or Hamburg. Unlike advertisers, however, they combine violent language with potential aggressiveness. Instead of soap, cigarettes and sweet, artificial drinks, Katharina Sieverding's art ostentatiously shows bombs and grenades. Astrid Klein, on the other hand, uses ghostly black-and-white photographs to contrast idyllic, flowery pictures of nature, with the unappetizing views of decaying inner cities. What is more, such pictures unmask the hidden mechanisms of what is gradually becoming an over-powerful public language – a language which has already gone beyond advertising, has begun to affect the

cinema and television and has grasped all areas of human existence within its embrace. The consequences of this language on the life of society are expressed with incisive clarity in the title of a widely read book by Neil Postman, *Amusing Ourselves to Death*.

However, anyone who has looked at Wegman's drawings, video films and photographs and thinks that this American artist is no more than a clownish buffoon, has failed to recognize the aesthetic explosiveness of his humorous pictures and the subversive power of his artistic imagination. Wegman used to parody Minimal and Concept Art, and the element of parody still dominates his art in the age of the post-avant-garde. In many ways Wegman was one of its forerunners. His art often reads like a satirical commentary on the development of contemporary art over the last 25 years. Wegman is one of those artists who have always been rather critical of the idea that art should be autonomous, even though he has never abandoned it, either. But what seems to be a contradiction is resolved in his use of parody. The American critic Craig Owen once drew attention to the element of dialogue inherent in parody. A parody converses, as it were, with the object of its satire, so that a work of art which mocks another speaks to the viewer in two different ways, i.e. the language of the work of art (the parody itself) and the language of the object which it pretends to imitate.

Wegman's art always spans several reference points, and these have increased in relation to the growth of reference points within art in general. Whereas avant-garde art was mainly concerned with itself, post-avant-garde art has been re-discovering the numerous facets of reality. Wegman has mastered the highly meaningful game of playing with different artistic reference points such as art and photography. His photographic work, in particular, is a mixture of the different principles which are inherent both in commercial and non-commercial art. Things that are similar come from backgrounds which appear to be dissimilar. People used to assume that art and fashion were incompatible, but in Wegman's art these have

Günther Förg:
Exhibition, Galerie Max Hetzler,
Cologne, October 1986

Jeff Wall:
The Drain, 1989
Cibacrometransparent, fluorescent light,
display case,
Image: 90 ¼ × 113 ⅝ in.
(229 × 288.5 cm)
Box: 98 × 121 ½ in.
(249 × 308.5 cm)
Galerie Johnen & Schöttle, Cologne

Page 183:

Jenny Holzer:
From the Survival Series, 1987
Installation in San Francisco
Barbara Gladstone Gallery, New York

merged into an indissoluble whole, with photography as the link between them. By satirizing fashion photography, he effectively undermines its dictatorial power while at the same time showing its influence on art. Fact and fiction, truth and imagination, are similarly mixed in his pictures. To compose his pictures, Wegman uses a large Polaroid camera – which enables the creator, or perhaps rather the "author", of the picture to exercise extremely accurate control over the result. The photographer becomes a painter, except that he does not actually use a paintbrush. With the camera lens, however, he is able to arrange a picture precisely, so that it suits his ideas. For an artist who is not a good craftsman but has plenty of taste and is well able to arrange a setting, this is the most suitable instrument. Has the gulf between photography and painting shrunk to the proportions of a mere technical problem? Wegman's photographic arrangements themselves are even more amazing, with ideas that have been borrowed both from fashion and advertising photography as well as art history. He combines highly symbolic visual stimuli with attractively fashionable clothes or transposes historical settings with certain fixed patterns of meaning into present-day contexts. His art is considerably more complex than it would seem to be at first sight, and it instils the viewer with a wish to try and interpret it. However, one needs to have a fairly good knowledge of imagery in order to find the thread that leads through Wegman's maze of images.

It should not really come as a surprise that even Neo-Figurative art has not remained unscathed by Wegman's assaults. Using a "pointed" paintbrush, the work which he has been

George Condo:
Conversation, 1983
Oil on canvas, 15¾ × 19⅝ in.
(40 × 50 cm)
Galerie Monika Sprüth, Cologne

EIN ÖFFENTLICHES
BAD
FÜR MÜNSTER

GEMALT VON THOMAS HUBER

creating since the mid-eighties parodies a type of painting that keeps an ironical distance from traditional art, while at the same time continuing it, albeit in a variety of different ways. Wegman even goes one step further and exposes the downright banality of many pictures with their powerful but pretentious claim to being art. What serves this purpose particularly well is his method of rendering perfect but routine art in a manner that is deliberately dilettantist.

Wegman has influenced a number of Dutch photographers whose theme is the image of world shown by photography. In real life the subjects of their works always look utterly unlike the photographs. A monumental piece of architecture, for instance, is no more than a tiny model, and the moon in Hocks's *Tramp* (1986) is only a mock-up or the built-in photographic reproduction of the real moon: it is held on a piece of string by a poorly clad figure who is sitting on a straw-covered wooden construction. And the bombastically framed photographs by Henk Tas, which appear to be stills from a mystery film by Steven Spielberg or George Lucas, are really only toy figures, carefully arranged in a "still life" for the camera. In 1987 the Groningen Museum, the most progressive Dutch museum of contemporary art, dedicated an entire exhibition to this specifically Dutch version of "arranged photography", and gave it the subtle title *Fotografia buffa*. The photographs exhibited were inspired by a number of different fields, including American slapstick films of the '30s and '40s, the graphic precision of comics, the wittiness of Magritte's Surrealism, an undisguised delight in parody and satire, as well as a deep feeling of suspicion towards the documentary function of photography. The title which the Dutch critics Linda Roodenberg and Hripsimé Visser chose for a programmatic article on Hocks's works was therefore quite logical, when it stated categorically that "Photography is not Authentic".

In West Germany it is artists like Martin Kippenberger, Albert Oehlen, Georg Herold and of course Milan Kunc who have been pursuing similar aims. Unlike their Dutch counterparts, however, their pictures tend to lack that slight touch of an almost British sense of humour. Tas and Hocks are in fact only two representatives of a larger artistic movement, and this, in turn, is very much part of that broad, general tendency called post-avant-garde. As such and with regard to artistic attitudes, methods and imagination, the movement is in many ways akin to

Thomas Huber:
Design for a Building-Site Poster ("A Public Swimming-Pool for Münster"), 1986
Oil on canvas, 59 × 100⅜ in.
(150 × 255 cm)
Galerie Philomene Magers, Bonn

Gerhard Merz:
Victory of the Sun MCMLXXXVII, 1987
Vittoria del sole MCMLXXXVII
Interior installation,
documenta 8, Kassel

Page 186:

Günther Förg:
Fall II, 1984
Sturz II
b/w photograph, framed,
70 ⅞ × 47 ⅜ in.
(180 × 120 cm)
Galerie Max Hetzler, Cologne

contemporary painting. After all, what these pictures are intended to undermine is people's collective ideas about the world, reality and human existence – ideas which have hardened into clichés, commonplace notions that reflect the mental stagnation of a society bent to maintain the status quo, a society that somehow seems to have become too slow and ponderous to change and which is now rushing headlong towards disaster. However, the fact that artists are unable to stop such a development does not absolve them from their duty to put up warning signs everywhere. But who takes such warnings seriously these days? Especially if artists are seen mainly in the role of buffoons. What can happen to such a buffoon has been illustrated extremely well in an anecdote by the Danish philosopher Kierkegaard, who summed up the situation more aptly than any profound sociological analysis: "It once happened that a fire broke out backstage in a theatre. The comedian came out to tell the public, and so people thought it was a joke and they applauded. He repeated his message, but people simply cheered all the louder. And I think this is how the world will perish, amidst the general cheers of fun-loving people who believe that it's all a joke."

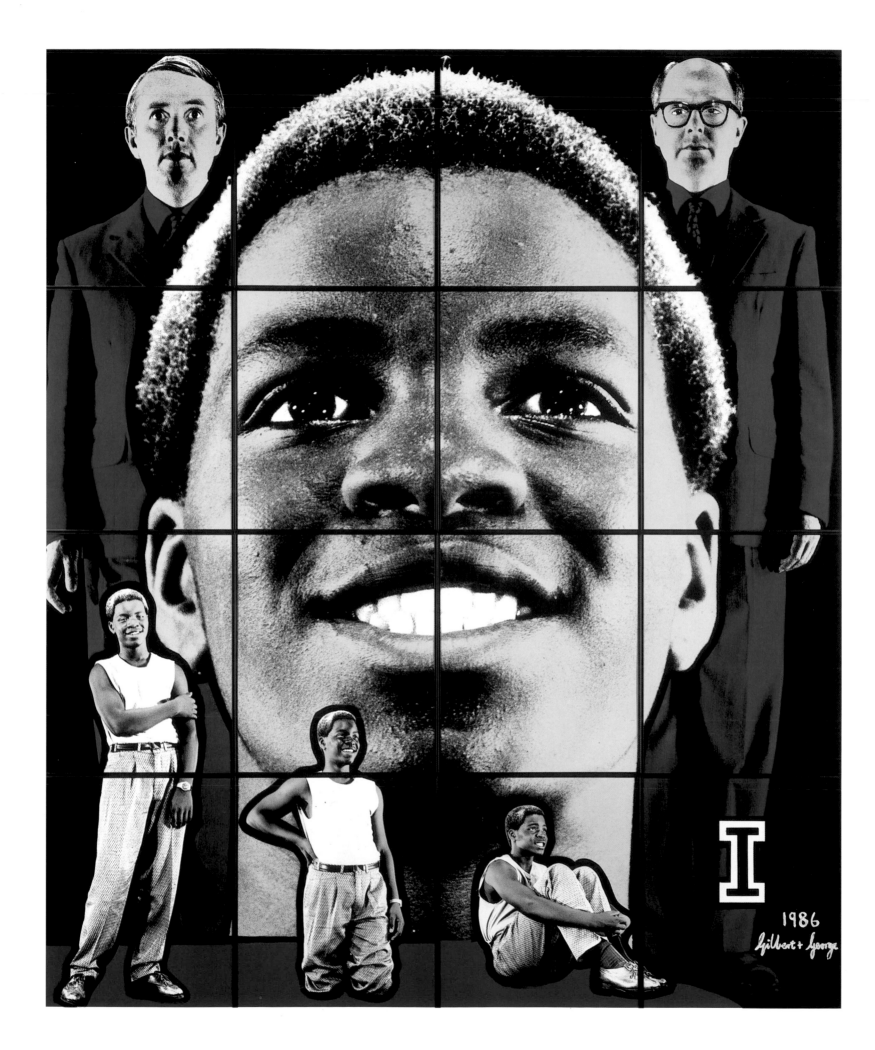

Loners or "Anything Goes"?

Once the doctrinaire positions of avant-garde art had been overcome, the contemporary art scene began to be so diverse and multi-faceted that the last periodic flickering of open attacks against dominating forms of art seemed rather unreal. After all, if there is anything one might want to deplore, then it is a certain randomness, the lack of any influential style or dominant artistic direction, and the lack of reliable signposts with regard to the further development of art. Again and again, instead of new approaches that might point to the future, artists apparently prefer to go back to artistic periods of the past, though not under the banner of unbroken continuity. Even the avant-garde – by now a historical phenomenon – has had its effect on contemporary art, and its lessons have by no means sunk into oblivion. And even today's successors to the avant-garde certainly recognize their duty to bow to the absolute claims of truth. It is a position that cannot be given up. In view of a world full of contradictions and inconsistencies there cannot be an art that tells of beauty and harmony, because such an art would be full of lies. Even artists who have chosen century-old artistic periods as their reference points continually emphasize their distance, both in form and content. And if – like the American artist Sherrie Levine – they choose to suspend this distance, then they do it in such an obvious way that their plagiarism can immediately be identified as plagiarism.

If montage was the most striking methodological principle at the beginning of our century, citation has taken its place at the end of it. The scope of these two methods, however, is not just a technical matter. There are points of contact between the two, and they also express some very striking spiritual and artistic attitudes. After the experience of the First World War, artists used montage techniques to put together the fragments of a world which had been shattered into many broken pieces, and so without trying to cover up the cracks, they created a new artistic unity. Artists nowadays use citations to call to mind what mankind and – by extension – art have irredeemably lost in the course of the 20th century. We live in a world that keeps oscillating between hope and fear, a world which has learnt to suppress its anxieties, even if these are repeatedly unleashed by every new disaster that is reported. In such a world the most convincing works of art are the ones that make us painfully aware of our loss, both physically and spiritually.

At the same time the art business has been seized by feverish and frenzied activity, and it seems occasionally as if the art market were continually propagating and launching new artistic movements, simply in order to conceal the loss which is documented in the art itself. The germ has already infected museums and art societies. Month after month one exhibition is followed by another, with a new art movement every season. For quite a while now even banks and insurance companies have been involved in the art market. Just as the famous fashion houses put new designs on the market every year, the art trade is now trying to promote new artistic styles.

Art has never been so much under the dictates of the laws of fashion, nor has it ever been so changeable. Unlike clothes, however, works of art are not perishables. For the keen observer of the art scene, who is not generally endowed with the gift of prophecy, they do not prove their worth as art until they have passed unscathed through several waves of fashion. This is what happens when an entire cultural configuration has emerged from behind the fleeting fancies of the various fashions, when the glamour has disappeared and made room for a vessel

James Lee Byars:
The Conscience, 1985
Guilded wood, glass dome, diameter of the
golden sphere, 1.06 in. (27 mm),
72⅞ × 22⅞ in. (185 × 58 cm)
Galerie Michael Werner, Cologne

Gilbert & George:
I, 1987
Photo-piece, 95¼ × 79½ in. (242 × 202 cm)
Anthony d'Offay Gallery, London

full of metaphorical meaningfulness that collects and condenses collective ideas and emotions in an exemplary way.

When the German philosopher Habermas so aptly describes the present situation as "new obscurity", then we can undoubtedly apply the same words to the contemporary art scene. In fact the very word *scene* is symptomatic enough. As on a stage, we can see the unfolding of a dramatic development, comical at times, a mixture of fact and fiction, with protagonists who often appear to be more important than that which they produce. Indeed, it is not just among the ranks of artists that certain stars have been born, but also among the entire host of critics. And even the organizers of those grand contemporary art spectacles have ascended to the heights of stardom – a small club whose members enjoy recommending themselves to one another and making more or less important statements about art. It is no coincidence that a lot of it seems like a kind of Hollywood on a smaller scale, less vulgar, and not quite as fascinating perhaps, but nevertheless oddly aloof, schematic and artificial. Small talk on art, with a glass of champagne in one hand. The art scene propagates a myth in which it is the most important participant. Looking with blasé eyes at the development of contemporary art, cynics cannot but conclude that "anything goes".

It has to be *neo*, however: *Neo-Geo*, a short revival of geometrical art, died as soon as the season had closed. The *documenta 8* exhibition in Kassel, more boring than ever before, seemed like an obituary. While a number of collectors simply ignored it, others hailed it with

John Armleder:
Untitled, 1987
Acrylic on canvas, with round table,
30 × 43¼ × 118⅛ in.
(76 × 150 × 300 cm)
Galerie nächst St. Stephan, Vienna

Helmut Federle:
Three Shapes, Two Crossed, 1985
Drei Formen zwei durchkreuzt
Dispersion on canvas, 82⅝ × 118⅛ in.
(210 × 300 cm)
Galerie nächst St. Stephan, Vienna

such fiery enthusiasm that prices began to soar. Nevertheless, Neo-Geo did succeed in elevating a number of artists to positions of well-deserved fame, such as the two Swiss artists John Armleder and Helmut Federle, as well as the Austrian Gerwald Rockenschaub. What distinguishes their art from the grand design of Constructivism in the 1920s is that their work lacks a utopian dimension, though not for any want of artistic ability. Rather, the artists have consciously decided to reject any form of utopianism in art. On the other hand, they do not feel offended if their art is described as decorative. Their pictures are delicately painted, with the highest degree of refinement, both in terms of form and colour. As works of art, they do not raise unusual problems of aesthetics, nor do they ask urgent questions about everyday life. Rockenschaub's small-format, exquisitely painted pictures and Federle's unobtrusive canvases, skilfully playing with the different nuances of adjacent colours, are superbly suited for decorating one's sitting-room – nor do they claim to be anything more than this. It would be wrong to scoff, because such art does, after all, indicate a remarkable change of direction. The most significant post-war artworks, from Abstract Expressionism to Neo-Figurative painting, were aimed, above all, at the public sector, i.e. the museums, rather than the private sphere. In fact, when we consider that a few decades ago museums were still seen as the epitome of drowsiness and stuffiness, it is quite remarkable that this honourable 19th century institution has experienced such an impressive worldwide revival over the last twenty years. Museums suddenly attract the hosts of visitors which football managers can only dream of. And so this rediscovery of geometrical art may possibly indicate a certain reorientation. Perhaps a turn towards man's inner self?

However, we should be very careful with such speculation, because even Armleder's art puts a damper on it. A mixture of paintings and reliefs, with obvious architectural references, it has the character of "open an work of art." (Umberto Eco) We always feel that we are facing the individual elements of a more comprehensive arrangement. Each work totally dominates the environment in which it has been placed. Armleder, one of the most popular artists in the second half of the eighties, used to make art furniture at one time, and together with the American artist Richard Artschwager he paved the way for an important variant of contemporary sculpture. Also, one can still detect traces of the significant tradition of Swiss Constructivism in his works, i.e. of artists like Max Bill and Camille Graeser, while the paintings of Federle and Rockenschaub show influences of Italian *arte concreta*.

The expressive paintings of Austrian and Swiss artists and the works of Rockenschaub, Federle, Armleder and others serve as mediators between the cultures of Northern and Southern Europe. Neo-Geo was an exception, because it never had a creative counterpart north of the Alps. A number of artists, on the other hand, met with considerably more enthusiasm. These were Siegfried Anzinger and Hubert Schmalix from Austria, Martin Disler and Miriam Cahn from Switzerland, and Leiko Ikemura, a Japanese artist who had first lived in Switzerland and then moved to West Germany. The sombreness of Anzinger's paintings, the translucent nudes in Schmalix's art, the obsessive eroticism in Disler's paintings, the note of thorough self-examination in Cahn and Ikemura's pictures – these are features which combine elements of Mediterranean and Nordic art, merging them in paintings that cultivate a seething mass of eccentric and controversial emotions. What is remarkable is that they have achieved this in spite of the obvious independence of their artistic

Philip Taaffe:
Untitled (Midnight Blue), 1985
Acrylic and collage on canvas,
76⅜ × 94⅞ in. (194 × 241 cm)
Private collection

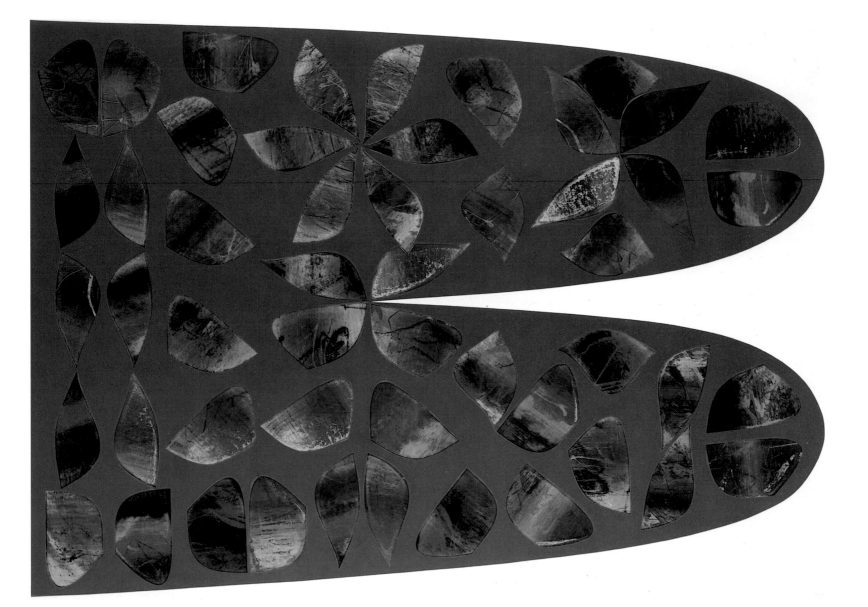

imagination and the cultural traditions of their respective countries. Owing to intelligently administered state subsidies, Austria in particular has developed into a cultural melting-pot, a country that can draw on its rich cultural heritage, without imperialist pretences, and which has extended its cultural horizon to encompass the adjacent European countries, north and south of its borders.

No sooner had Neo-Geo been established, than the American art scene began to awaken from its creative lethargy, and Manhattan – throbbing with life – started to mobilize entire hosts of fresh artists. However, even their art can far more easily be defined in terms of overall artistic attitudes on which it is based than any typical stylistic features that one might find in the individual works. This makes it rather difficult to find a suitable term to summarize them, and *Neo-Conceptual Art* must be regarded as no more than a temporary term. Jerry Saltz, one of the American promoters of this artistic trend, has described the artists' attitude as "realistic": "Although the works often seem abstract, they are never without subjects. Rather, abstraction here combines with concrete physical and social forms of everyday life, thus showing signs of a 'new realism', which is nearly always formulated with a view directed to the outside world, rather than one's inner self, a realism whose objective can be to comment on the consumer society, the abuse of art, the role of the artist, the progress of technology, the loss of political ideals or cultural criticism. A form of 'realism', in other words, which has nothing to do with 'depiction'."

And in fact the realism of these American artists does indeed express itself above all in their general attitudes, particularly towards contemporary art and the art market. They have found their own way of adopting the cynical motto, "Anything goes". Sherrie Levine has been

Philip Taaffe:
Nativity (Red White), 1986
Screenprint collage and acrylic on canvas,
64 × 88⅝ in. (162.5 × 225 cm)
Galerie Paul Maenz, Cologne

particularly consistent in this respect, because she paints and photographs only pictures which she actually likes. The resulting works often bear a striking resemblance to pictures which already exist. The modern corpus from which she selects the material for her "games" ranges from Schiele and Malewitch to the photographer Walker Evans and the painter Brice Marden. She uses these resources with self-confidence, changes their striking individual "images" (for that is how they are mostly perceived), and by re-adapting their most characteristic features, establishes an ironical distance between her own works and the original paintings. Like many of her American colleagues, Sherrie Levine has been inspired by French theoreticians. She understands her work as a kind of visual "deconstruction", to quote Jacques Derrida. At first sight, this may seem like downright plagiarism, but it is in fact a highly sensitive and theoretically sound attempt to enable us to look at certain works of art with fresh eyes, to restore to a level of new innocence those works which – to paraphrase Marlene Dietrich's words – have been reproduced "to death".

Jeff Koons, who digs deeper into art history than Sherrie Levine, derives his inspiration from the Baroque. His witty miniature sculptures are reminiscent of Benvenuto Cellini's, whose most famous piece of work was his salt barrel for King François I. Koons has updated Cellini's artistic programme, while at the same time, of course, making it more rudimentary. His group of stainless steel sculptures derives its impact from the inappropriateness of the form taken to convey their artistic message. There is a discrepancy between form and content, whereby the main artistic problem is pushed onto a semiological level. Thus Koons provokes a discussion of the position of art in Western society. In a world where everything is measured in terms of money, the important difference between an old work of art and a contemporary one is merely a matter of price. Therefore, he was only being consistent when he devoted himself to the products of modern industrial design after his "retrophase."

Leo Castelli, the Nestor of the American art trade and the most influential art dealer for over thirty years, represents the works of Koon's colleague Meyer Vaisman. On the occasion of Castelli's eightieth birthday an interview was published in a West German newspaper in

Top left:

Jeff Koons:
Two Balls 50/50 Tank
Glass, iron, water, basketballs
Sonnabend Gallery, New York

Top right:

Jeff Koons:
New Hoover Convertibles, New Shelton Wet/
Dry, Displaced Double-Decker, 1981-87
Perspex, vacuum cleaner, fluorescent light
99 × 41 × 28 in.
(251.5 × 104.1 × 71.1 cm)
Sonnabend Gallery, New York

which the art dealer spoke extremely highly of Meyer Vaisman. The artist has summarized the most diverse decorative tendencies in his works and created a synthesis with his paintings and objects in which the most incompatible aesthetic poles within avant-garde art merge almost naturally – whether these poles are abstract or representational, historical or contemporary, traditional or progressive.

Then there is Haim Steinbach who has created the most amazing installations by using simple, everyday objects, such as metal walking frames for elderly people, without altering their original designs. He is a belated successor of Marcel Duchamp, the *spiritus rector* of radical avant-garde, and a spiritual kinsman of the German sculptor Reinhard Mucha. It is obvious, at any rate, that he has a great sense for surprising combinations that spark off witty ideas and skilfully blend the maxim of the "ready-made" in art with forms from modern industrial design.

What is unsettling about these artists is the conspicuous element of playfulness. One misses the thread or the artist's personal handwriting, his style or – commercially speaking – his trademark. The artists roam about in art history, both ancient and modern, using, in a practical way, whatever they find interesting or fascinating. However, unlike the art students of the 19th and 20th century academies, they vary these images instead of copying them. Philip Taaffe first imitated paintings by Arnold Newman and Bridget Riley and created mere paraphrases, before ridding himself of the fetters of such mimesis and using – as an American art critic put it – more "polyglot" formulations in his art. He simply loves ornamental compositions, and this may well be the reason why, until now, he has avoided any tendency towards sheer randomness in his artistic methods. After all, sweeping eclecticism is the most striking feature of this artistic wave, which is now beginning to flow over from the States to Europe. Many American artists have been riding on this wave, including Ashley Bickerton, Peter Schuyff (who adores a decorative geometry), Steinbach, Annette Lenieux and Peter Halley, who are probably the most original artists.

Is this the artistic trend with which American artists are now trying to regain ground in the

European art scene? The German art dealer Paul Maenz, who dramatically rang in the nineties by withdrawing from the gallery scene, certainly seemed to be convinced of it: "For almost ten years now the scene has been dominated by young Europeans, particularly Italians and Germans, even in the U.S. From Clemente to Dokoupil an entire world of profoundly European ideas has been emerging which can by now be regarded as the art of the eighties. There seems to be hardly anything typically American that might correspond to the rich variety of these continuously influential paintings. In the meantime a young art scene has begun to take shape in New York. It may be true that their art is in many ways a reaction to the dominant position of so many Europeans, but their impact is undoubtedly a result of that direct way in which they tackle certain phenomena of everyday life. These phenomena are typical of American lifestyle and American culture." The first large-scale presentation of Neo-Conceptualism on the European continent took place in Madrid and Barcelona and was given the characteristic title *Art as its Own Double*. Does the motto "Anything goes" really mean the total rejection of artistic creativity and imagination? Does it mean that only citations, imitations and replicas will prevail in the future? Many questions will have to remain unanswered. On the other hand, however, this obvious bewilderment, which cannot be concealed behind frantic activity, affords the wholesome option of stopping in one's tracks, of re-thinking and examining oneself. If mainstream art is no longer an enormous torrent which pulls everything along and drowns all critical reservations, then the tributaries may once again begin to attract attention, and so can their contribution to the development of art in general.

Bill Woodrow:
Still Waters, 1985
3 car bonnets, 3 spring mattresses, enamel and acrylic, 54 × 122 × 245 in.
(137.2 × 309.9 × 622.3 cm)
Museum of Contemporary Art,
La Jolla/California

Haim Steinbach:
Untitled, 1987
Wall object, gold, silver, mixed media,
62¾ × 89¾ × 26½ in.
(159.5 × 228 × 67.5 cm)
FER Collection

It may be true that every cultural phenomenon owes its existence to a whim of fashion. But it would be totally misguided to conclude that the opposite also holds, i.e. that every fashion contains a force which is culturally creative. What can happen is that a certain fashion may suddenly shift existing cultural achievements into the dazzling limelight of public interest, even though they have been taking place largely in obscurity. As a result, the fashion itself is given lasting support, and the cultural achievement is finally assessed according to its true value. Such a development is always of considerable benefit to cultural outsiders.

Art history has always known artists who refused to be pigeon-holed in any of the great styles, from Hieronymus Bosch and Francisco de Goya to Edouard Manet and Francis Bacon. With regard to artistic quality it is irrelevant whether an artist has had a decisive influence on the development of mainstream art or whether his art combines an equal amount of old and new, of traditional and innovative elements. To the extent, however, that art is becoming more and more subject to the dictates of fashion, there is also an increasing tendency among artists to reclaim for themselves the position of lone wolves.

Even artists whose work has given them the image of lone wolves and outsiders do not live in a vacuum outside history. As a rule, they are far more deeply rooted in artistic tradition than their colleagues, although this certainly does not detract from their topical nature. It is characteristic of the present situation in contemporary art that almost an entire field within the spectrum of artistic options seems to have severed its links with mainstream art. This is the art of sculpture. Most sculptors are still vehemently defending the principle of artistic autonomy, and there is only a handful of younger artists (such as Reinhard Mucha, Siah Armajani, Stephan Huber, Hubert Kecol, Scott Burton, Franz West, Ludger Gerdes and Thomas Schütte) who, in line with Post-Modern architecture, are endeavouring to create sculptures which are appropriate to specific places and environments. The most prominent contemporary sculptors on the side of autonomous art are Richard Serra and Ulrich Rück-

riem, whose works are neither avant-garde nor post-avant-garde. Serra's menacing steel constructions and Rückriem's bulky blocks of stone are as erratic in the landscape of contemporary art as they are in the interior or exterior spaces of their actual environments. They resist all attempts to categorize them, and above all they are not prepared to yield to any kind of circumstances. Serra and Rückriem are extremely sensitive in their work, and they meet the challenges of a given space with a good deal of precision. Nevertheless, they always create dominant signs, which makes them the last convincing representatives of the monumental principle in sculpting.

It may be due to the bulkiness of their material that – compared with painters and photographers – sculptors have always been considerably slower in reacting to the promptings of that much-quoted *zeitgeist*. Whereas figurative elements have been gaining ground in painting for a number of years now, they are still being resisted by most sculptors. It is true that non-abstract tendencies have been getting more frequent in contemporary sculptures recently, such as in the works of the British sculptors Richard Deacon and Anish Kapoor, and there is obviously a new willingness to revive the severed dialogue with nature. This was demonstrated quite emphatically at the *documenta 8* exhibition, at *Skulptur* in Münster and parallel projects in Essen, Antwerp and Amsterdam, and above all – a year earlier – at Sonsbeek Park in Holland. But a lot of those sculptures still seem either too playful or too half-hearted or too contrived to shake the artistic position of someone like Serra or Rückriem.

Rückriem's numerous public sculptures, in particular, keep a very convincing balance between a claim to autonomy and a sensitive response to the actual sites. "Ulrich Rückriem has an internationally undisputed position among German sculptors. In fact, he is a classical sculptor, in the proper sense of the word: he goes to the quarry, picks out his stones with his own hands, and instead of chiselling an alien shape out of them, he extracts the intrinsic, essential value from the rough block of stone, either by determining the best possible area to

Reinhard Mucha:
Wind and Towers, Too High, 1982
Wind und zu hohe Türme
Interior installation
Saatchi Collection, London

Page 199:

Reinhard Mucha:
The Figure-Ground Problem of Baroque Architecture (The Only Thing that is Left for You is the Grave), 1985
Das Figur-Grundproblem in der Architektur des Barock (für dich allein bleibt nur das Grab)
Interior installation
Musée Nationale d'Art Moderne,
Centre Georges Pompidou, Paris

Hubert Kiecol:
Clinker Sculpture, 1983
Klinkerskulptur
clinker, 70⅞ in. (180 cm) high
Galerie Max Hetzler, Cologne

split an untouched surface or by polishing it and thus exposing the inner character of the stone. His craftsmanship can be seen in the way he breaks and cuts the stone, while his artistic skills lie in the balancing and proportioning of the sides to one another in its purest form." (Georg Jappe)

Rückriem will probably influence the future of sculpting in the same way that Polke and Richter will have an influence on painting. Rückriem's excellent craftsmanship and artistic feeling for the hidden "soul" of the material, his intuitively secure sense of shape and his strong creative urge mark him as an outstanding representative of his craft. As a "classical" sculptor, who maintains the balance between secure craftsmanship and a clear, simple, and elementary language of shapes, Rückriem is indeed a loner in contemporary art. His art rises high above the waves of fashion and has struck a happy medium between grand abstraction and that grand realism of Kandinsky. It "embodies", as it were, a certain artistic earthiness and therefore a direct complement to the excessive intellectual classicism of artists like Constantin Brancusi.

In painting, the revival of an expressive and representational art meant that the extraordinary works of a number of painters could now come to the fore. These painters had been largely overshadowed by the avant-garde, i.e. Frank Auerbach and Lucien Freud (Britain), Antonius Höckelmann and Karl Marx (West Germany), Guttuso (Italy), Pearlstein and Alex Katz (U.S.), and of course the "Big Four" from East Germany, Willi Sitte, Bernhard Heisig, Berner Tübke and Wolfgang Matthäuer. Even Bacon's impressive oeuvre is beginning to emerge from obscurity again. These painters had already achieved a considerable amount of fame in their own countries, but – with the exception of Bacon – they did not become internationally renowned until the post-avant-garde. The situation was rather different in Marx's case, though, because the West German discussion of his art was quite heated before

Hubert Kiecol:
Column on its Side, 1987
Säule Liegend
Concrete, three parts, 16½ × 23⅜ × 9½ in.
(42 × 60 × 24 cm)
Galerie Max Hetzler, Cologne

he was given his well-deserved recognition as an artist. Even though Marx is not a "classical" painter, his paintings do include a considerable number of traditional features, both with regard to technique and structure. There is very little in contemporary art that might match the eroticism of his paintings. What irritates quite a few people is Marx's combination of high artistic standards and aggressively obscene subject matter. Like Bacon and Pearlstein, Marx is an obsessive painter whose aesthetic mind revolves almost exclusively around the ancient problem of *eros* (sexual love) and *thanatos* (death). His dramatic paintings reflect the provocative ideas of George Bataille, who sees nature as an extraordinary machine that permanently "feeds" on death and decay. Death is the price of life! And with subjects like this, his pictures seem even more alien than Bacon's paintings, which tell of loneliness and despair.

In this respect Höckelmann seems to be on a similar spiritual wavelength. His effervescent series of phantoms illustrate the idea of nature as a *natura naturans*, i.e. constantly growing, giving birth to itself and, if necessary, taking the most cruel revenge whenever man encroaches too far on its territory. Höckelmann's paintings and sculptures are therefore more "realistic" than the fruitless artistic lamentations about a possible worldwide natural disaster. Höckelmann, too, is a loner in contemporary art, who refuses to yield to the laws of fashion or to any collective group strategies. Being of the same generation as Baselitz and one of the precursors of the "miraculous Berlin artists", he has always pursued his aims independently of others and has never obeyed the determining communal spirit of any particular art gallery.

In this context we must mention two further artists, Gilbert & George, who, despite their obstinacy, have been able to hold their own in the established art world, and also one outsider, Boltanski, who left a well-known gallery, developed his career in art societies and museums, and who can be understood as representing numerous others. Gilbert & George

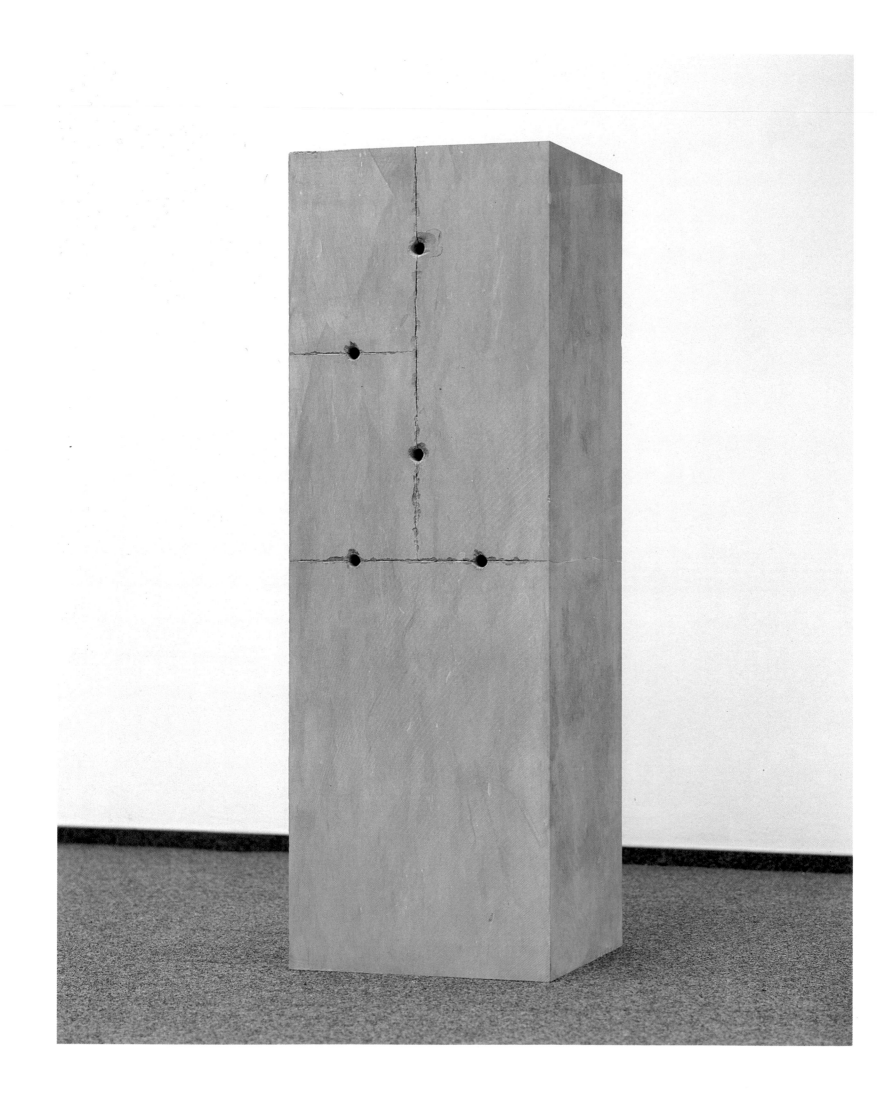

Top left:

Ulrich Rückriem:
Untitled, 1986
Stone, split, cut and re-assembled in its original
shape, 68⅞ × 88⅝ × 17¾ in.
(175 × 225 × 45 cm)

Top right:

Ulrich Rückriem:
From a four-part interior installation, 1986
Granite (Bleu de Vir, Normandy), split, cut
and re-assembled in its original shape,
78¾ × 78¾ × 13¾ in.
(200 × 200 × 35 cm)

Page 202:

Ulrich Rückriem:
Pillar, since 1986
Upright dolomite, cut on all sides and
re-assembled in its original shape,
19⅝ × 59 × 19⅝ in. (50 × 150 × 50 cm)

started their career as "living sculptures": like puppets in a musical clock they would perform a figure of eight, dancing the same dance hour after hour. Also, they have managed to gain important positions in the contemporary art scene as active critics of the capitalist system. In fact, they are themselves the crystallized figures which appear in their gigantic tableaux, photographic montages, paintings and writing, a depressing panorama of social conditions and their psychological effects. As violent as real life, their art is shrill, cynical and relentless.

Boltanski's strategy, on the other hand, is more subtle and subversive. He is a modern magician. Like Gilbert & George, Boltanski has survived unscathed the numerous changes in artistic styles, and he also enjoys making use of photography, without necessarily seeing himself as a photographer. What he shares with Marx, though probably not even consciously, is a yearning for death. It is, however, mainly the mechanisms of our modern world with their technology, such as electrical light and photography, which have stimulated Boltanski. His art is full of death symbols: hidden chambers (at the *documenta 8* exhibition in Kassel) and grottos (shortly afterwards, in Amsterdam) are furnished with photographs of children or electrical streamers of light, reminding us of the catacombs of the early Christians. His works combine individual and collective experiences, and no contemporary artist neutralizes the glossy aestheticism of commercial photography as impressively as Boltanski. He merely emphasizes the simple fact that every photograph is a memento mori – a contemporary variant of the old still life.

Michael Buthe is another loner among contemporary artists. The artistic universe which he has created for himself is an entirely personal one, a universe that consists of dreams and fairly-tales, borrowed from foreign cultures and from the clichés of Western civilization. In order to really discover Buthe's artistic world, one has to immerse oneself in it completely and entrust oneself entirely to its inexpressible magic. Buthe, too, seems to be some kind of magician, but one from a different world.

However, there is a group of painters who are not so much loners, but nevertheless – still – outsiders. These are the women. It is of course true that Pattern & Decoration had meant a tremendous boost to the value of feminine sensitivity in the world of art, and a number of women had made a name for themselves by making use of technological media (Cindy Sherman, Katharina Sieverding and Astrid Klein, and above all the two Americans Jenny Holzer and Barbara Kruger). But when artists began to paint again at the beginning of the

Frank Stella:
Sinjerli Variation II, 1986
Acrylic on canvas, 120 in. (305 cm)
in diameter
Galerie Strelow, Düsseldorf

Frank Stella:
Corpo-senza-l'anima, 1987
Paint on aluminium
130 × 116 × 59½ in.
(330.2 × 294.6 × 151 cm)
Galerie Strelow, Düsseldorf

Robert Gober:
Three Urinals, 1988
Wood, wire lath, plaster, enamel paint,
21 ¾ × 15 ¼ × 15 in.
(55.2 × 38.8 × 38 cm) each,
21 ¾ × 73 ¼ × 15 in.
(55.2 × 186.1 × 38 cm) overall
Paula Cooper Gallery, New York

Page 207

Robert Gober:
Untitled, 1985-87
Plaster, wire lath, wood,
semi glass, enamel,
24 × 24 × 20 in.
(60.96 × 60.96 × 50.8 cm)
Collection S.I. Newhouse, Jr., New York

Anish Kapoor:
1000 Names, 1981
Wood, plaster of Paris and pigment,
42 × 64 in.
(106.6 × 162.7 cm)
Lisson Gallery, London

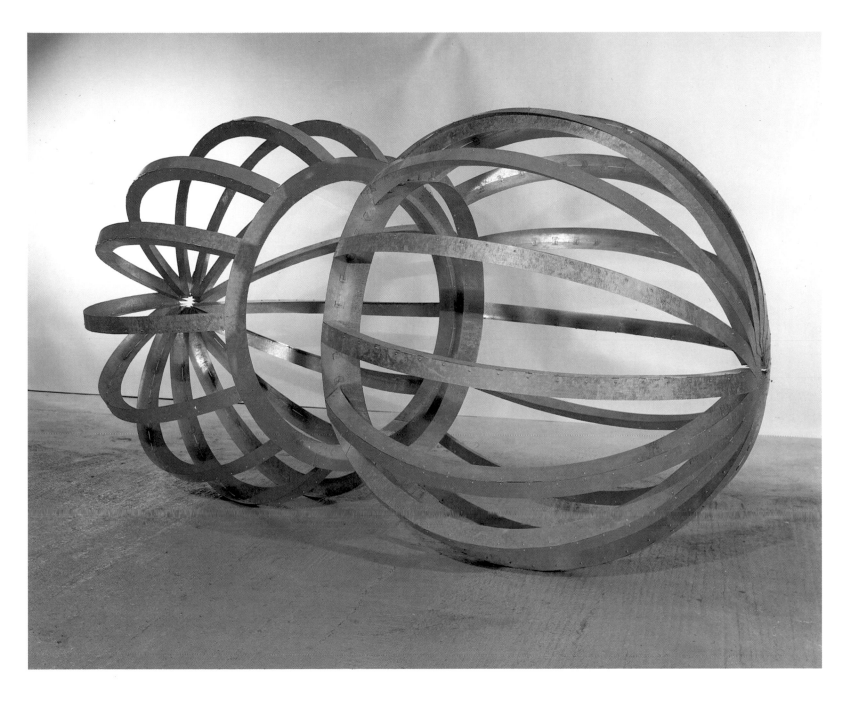

Richard Deacon:
Two Can Play, 1983
Galvanized steel, 72 × 144 × 72 in.
(183 × 365.8 × 183 cm)
Lisson Gallery, London

Meyer Vaisman:
Four Small Fillers, 1987
Canvas on wooden frames,
180¼ × 72 × 11¼ in. (458 × 183 × 28.5 cm)
Galerie Paul Maenz, Cologne

eighties, this changed the situation at one fell stroke. "Real" art suddenly seemed to be a male prerogative again. Neither in Italy nor in France, Austria or Holland did any woman painters emerge who might deserve consideration, though the situation was slightly different in Switzerland, the U.S. and West Germany.

The careers of two German artists, Isa Genzken, one of Richter's students, and Rosemarie Trockel, a trained painter, are particularly characteristic of a certain tendency in contemporary art. Both artists began to attract people's attention with some rather extraordinary sculptures, full of references to the real world. This is all they have in common, but both artists have indeed remained outsiders rather than loners in the art world, even though their works manifest some fairly typical artistic attitudes which are prevalent in the period leading up to the turn of the millenium. This is particularly true for Rosemarie Trockel. Her art derives its inspiration from the post-avant-garde and shows a spiritual kinship with the works of other artists of her generation, such as Dahn. However, her art is less playful, less ironical in the way it delivers its messages and less of a tightrope walk. It is more serious, and in many ways also more committed, and it is shot through with a very strong erotic element. Rosemarie Trockel has an obsessive love of drawing, she has used all kinds of techniques and tools, including pencils, ballpoint pens, water-colours and gouache, and there seems to be no limit to her inexhaustible imagination. Her subjects are mainly taken from her own, personal experience, although she has confidently turned this into something more general. There is a bodily warmth about them, a physical intimacy, which partly succeeds in making up for the loss of the physical aspect in present-day art. Her sculptures, on the other hand, unmistakably speak of losses, as they continually revolve around the subject of death. They are usually vessels shaped like urns or mussels, apparently protecting new life – or life that is coming to an end – from the clutches of death. Her preferred subject was, at one stage, the human skull in all its awesome beauty. A few years ago, however, Rosemarie Trockel began to take an interest in painting, and with the exception of a small number of pictures – which include a

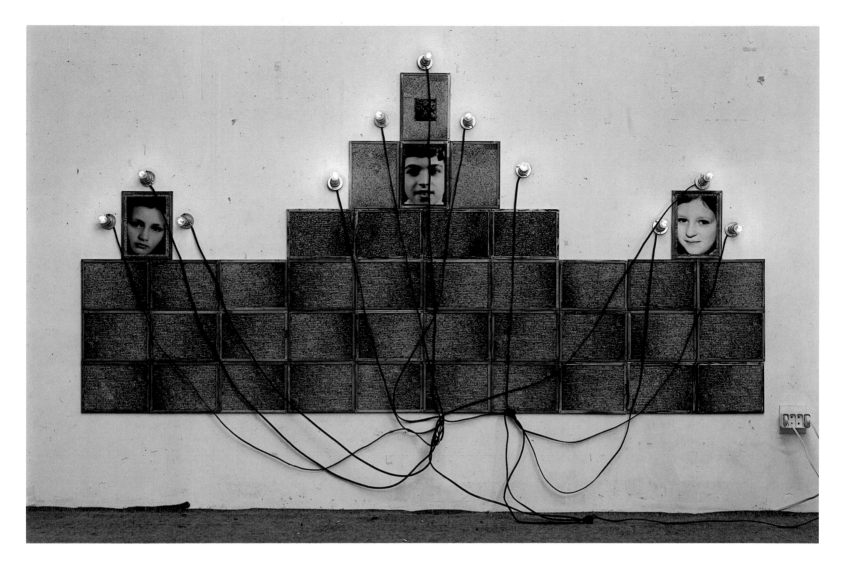

Christian Boltanski:
Monument,1986
Interior installation

self-portrait reminiscent of the portrait style of the Renaissance – the motifs chosen are completely unlike the ones in her drawings and sculptures. Whereas the latter were from the area of personal experience and had an intimately erotic aura about them, the subjects in her paintings come from the public sphere. She uses a wide variety of different emblems, ranging from the *Playboy* bunny to the international pure-wool seal and the Soviet hammer and sickle, which she arranges in entire series across the pictures. These are not so much paintings as pictures produced with knitting machines and according to the artist's programmatic instructions – anonymous signs which symbolize man's alienation, as well as a loss of clarity and emotional warmth. Rosemarie Trockel arranges them in a depressingly uniform rhythmic pattern, while at the same time using a type of material that suggests warmth and protection and therefore emphasizing even more the discrepancy between the subject and its artistic expression. Since Beuys no artist has shown so much intuitive feeling for the specific qualities of materials as Rosemarie Trockel.

Isa Genzken is, like many other female artists, a loner *par excellence* - a quality which she shares with Rebecca Horn, Shirazeh Houshiary, Marisa Merz, Ulrike Rosenbach, Susanne Solano, Marianne Eigenheer and of course Hanne Darboven. This makes it difficult to categorize her art in terms of any particular movement, and it is probably true to say that her kind of art could only have been produced at this time of profound and far-reaching revolutionary change. What strikes the eye immediately is the contrast between the material and the shapes of her sculptures, i.e. the breathtaking elegance and lightness of her wooden sculptures and the unfinished appearance of those made of concrete. Isa Genzken's contribution to the sculpture exhibition in Münster was a large concrete gate which summarized the formal structure of its environment, while at the same time seeming to criticize it by dint of its lightness and its temporary character. So although Isa Genzken has taken up the thread of the avant-garde, she has foiled its doctrinaire elementarism by giving it an appearance of transitoriness. What is more, the fragile nature of her ferroconcrete sculptures and the

Isa Genzken:
Corridor (Side View), 1986
Painted concrete, 32⅞ × 16⅛ × 11⅞ in.

Richard Serra:
Street Level, 1987
5 steel plates, 196 × 410 × ⅛in. each,
altogether: 196 × 820 × 410 in.
documenta 8, Kassel

lightness of her wooden sculptures make her art seem like counter-projects compared with traditional sculpture. This makes Isa Genzken's art modern, but without any fashionable modern trappings. The artist has succeeded in preserving the unalienable principles of the avant-garde for the cultural development of the present.

Finally, it seems appropriate to ask what will be the final destiny of art – an art which is more pluralistic than ever. What are the important landmarks? Perhaps Isa Genzken's fragile and sensitive sculptures, or Rückriem's "classical" works? The quotations of American artists, with all their eclecticism, or the Neo-Classicist projects of people like Gerhard Merz and Ludger Gerdes? The "Baroque" spatial constructions of Mucha or the enticingly colourful sculptures of Kapoor? The large-format photographs of Katharina Sieverding or Förg's photo-installations - a mixture of photography, painting and architecture? And what about painting itself? Will it give way to sculpting and architecture, just as years before it yielded its place to photography?

And it is true that on the threshold of the next milennium there ist not much happening in painting. No innovative endeavours are taking shape and there is a growing impression that this expressive artistic medium so rich in tradition has been exhausted for the time being. There are occasional paintings that surprise us, by established artists for the most part or by others, such as Jürgen Klauke, who had not tried their hand at painting before. Klauke's pictures in decadently poisonous colours evoke the moods and images of a world that is in many ways threatened and also threatening itself; amidst the hectic carnival bustle, this handwriting on the wall is strangely out of keeping with the times. For, unlike 100 years ago, it is not the strains of fin-de-siècle elegy, but rather sheer optimism that is the order of the day. Undaunted by stock *market* crashes, Europeans and Americans are looking to the future with great expectations. On the other hand, given the perceptible lack of orientation in the art of the Western hemisphere, the thematic painting of East German and Soviet origin has taken on an unanticipated persuasive power. Ever since the extremely successful comprehensive exhibition in Los Angeles (1989), the trademark 'German art' is no longer exclusively identified, even in the United States, with art from West Germany. The names of the originators of that style of painting cultivated in the East are still relatively unknown beyond Germany's borders; but given the momentum of the process aimed at unifying the two German states, inevitably set into motion by the radical political change which took place in

Asta Gröting:
The Happy Marriage, 1989
Die glückliche Ehe
b/w photograph, 8 ⅝ × 6 in.
(21.9 × 15.5 cm)
Galerie Isabella Kacprzak, Cologne

Page 213:

Richard Serra:
Terminal, 1976/77
Steel, four plates, 12.3 m high
documenta 6, Kassel

East Germany in October and November 1989, there can be no doubt that names such as Heisig, Tübke and Mattheuer, or Volker Stelzmann, Hartwig Ebersbach, Arno Rink and Michael Morgner as well as that of sculptor Trak Wendisch will shine like stars in the heavens of contemporary art in future. Perfect command of the painter's craft, social commitment, a relatively high degree of legibility and internal structures which are reflective of the artistic experience in the age of modernity have earned this conscious form of narrative painting attention and respect. It has taken its place in the spectrum of 'German painting'.

European photography has also been affected by decisive new impulses from East German photographers and artists. Thomas Florschuetz, who moved to the West even before the wall was opened up, has become a serious challenger to established artist-photographers and photographic artists with his unique photographic combinations of super-enlarged detail shots of his own body. His compelling photographic ensembles take photography to a level of intensity that would not have been thought possible. Emerging from the shadows of the wall are still other chroniclers of the socio-psychological sensibilities of a society under the yoke of Eastern-bloc socialism. As serious-minded as they are talented, the works of East German artists have supported a discernable tendency in West German freelance photography which is aimed at achieving a sharper focus on reality than has been the case in documentary photography of the past. It comes to light in the photo-images of Thomas Ruf, Thomas Struth, Axel Hütte, Candida Höfer and Andreas Gursky, including pupils of Bernhard Becher, in particular. Together with his wife Hilla, Becher has finally resolved the conflict which existed between art and photography for nearly a century with methodical comparisons of photograhic images. The Bechers have combined aesthetic principles of contemporary art such as seriality and multifocality with the clarity characteristic of the language of neo-

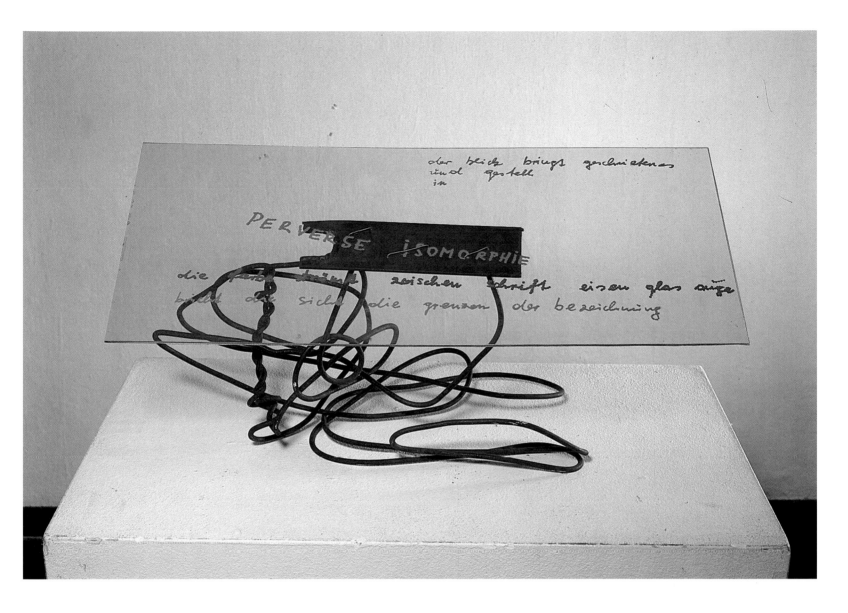

Franz West:
Isomorphism, 1986
Glass and wire, 22½ × 12⅝ × 13 in.
(57 × 32 × 33 cm)
Galerie Peter Pakesch, Vienna

objective photographic imagery. The amazing combination of realistic visual reproduction and aesthetic reflexion is a symptomatic feature of the influential Becher School. It has liberated photography from the confines of one-dimensional representational realism and promoted its documentary offshoot to the status of a legitimate art form.

Now that art has given up its reserve vis-à-vis photography and mastered it on a broad scale, with a resulting flood of examples of imaginative and at times cleverly staged photographic realities, the growing influence of the Becher School and of photographic artists such as Förg signals a reawakened interest in the manifold manifestations of empirical reality, a reality which can be seen and experienced. Reality returns to the referential system of art. A further indication of this development is the surprising attention which is suddenly being given to historical themes in contemporary art. It is no coincidence that the return of history to art has found most eloquent expression in Germany. The Renaissance theoretician Leon Batista Alberti had celebrated the art of painting historical scenes as the highest discipline and his assessment was still supported by the academic painters of the last century. Nevertheless, when the avant-garde swept the scene, the heyday of this genre came to an abrupt end. When East German painting first began to reflect historical events, it was regarded in the West as evidence of aesthetic backwardness. In the meantime, this has proved to be a rash judgement. Historical themes have provided important motifs not only for Kiefer's paintings, photographic works, sculptures and environments – and even a complete airplane hangar at the farewell exhibition of the Galerie Maenz; they have also found their way into the aesthetic works of a generation of artists who were not known for having any great inclination to portray historical scenes. Förg makes fairly frequent use of historical signs, as do Büttner and Oehlen; emininently historical problems appear encoded in Herold's work, and in that of the

Leon Golub:
Mercenaries VI, 1987
Acrylic on canvas, 120 × 146 in.
(304.8 × 370.8 cm)
Barbara Gladstone Gallery, New York

Karl Marx:
Man with Shadow, Self-Portrait, 1982
Mann mit Schatten, Selbstbildnis
Acrylic on canvas, 78¾ × 98½ in.
(200 × 250 cm)

photo-artists Klein and Rudolf Bonvie, and history has left its mark on the works of older artists such as Marx and Wolf Vostell as well. Even Richter invoked history with a moving cycle of paintings on the Baader-Meinhoff complex, for which he even resurrected painting techniques he had not used for a long time. With this group of works, he was able to pull off an extraordinary experiment: His technique of blurring clearcut photorealistic lines proved to be the only appropriate means of aesthetically coping with a subject as contradictory and repressed in West German minds as the events surrounding the founders of the Red Army Fraction (RAF). And he was able to do so without playing down its political importance or betraying it to superficial speculation and the addiction to topicality. As a critical antithesis to the undifferentiated glut of information from the mass media, art aims once more to fulfil what is – also – its social function.

This is particularly true of Hanne Darboven's work, which is genuinely universal. It is like a block that rises erratically from the midst of a pluralistic art scene which is shot through with mediocrities and trivialities. And it is captivating in its aesthetic intelligence, formal precision, disciplined imagination and abundance of visual content, which is utterly overwhelming. Darboven forges a cultural-historical panorama of incomparable niveau in contemporary art. She composes drawings in the widest variety of written forms, arranged in a systematic sequence which obeys a special mathematical principle, and combines them with photographic images and effectively chosen finds from everyday culture. The drawings function as the musical scores for a profound philosophy of the times which, however, never loses its concrete quality in abstraction, but rather feeds the observer's mental images with concrete-sensory materiality. Darboven also opened up the pictorial arts to the realm of sound by allowing a series of groups of graphic works to be converted into notes. Thus a unique aesthetic construct emerged, with a lucid sensuous aura and intellectual depth, one of the most ambitious attempts in contemporary art to meet the complicated world artistically and aesthetically with adequate means.

While the young public in Europe is discovering Pop Art – the 'art of consumption,' as it

C.O. Paeffgen:
Untitled (Queen), 1972
Acrylic on photo canvas, 43¼ × 70⅞ in.
(110 × 180 cm)
Dietmar Werle, Cologne

Amandus Hackelmann
The Newspaper Reader, 1985-87
Der Zeitungsleser
Indian ink and coloured wax crayons on paper,
39⅜ × 54¾ in. (100 × 139 cm)
Galerie Zimmer, Düsseldorf

were (on some days of the Warhol retrospective, the Ludwig Museum in Cologne reminded one of the main station in Cologne on the first day of summer holiday) – the artworld is breathing new life into the ideas, aesthetic principles and strategies of minimalist art and the cerebral Conceptual Art of the seventies. It is now the American artists who emphasize the primacy of the artistic idea, although the American mentality is contradictory to an artistic praxis of this orientation. The works of Koons, Bickerton, Halley and Mike Kelley as well as Christopher Wool and Luise Lawler follow in the tired traditions of the European and American avant-garde, but without being able to provide them with fresh impulses of any lasting effect. They usually content themselves with more or less intelligent variations, which are played up by zealous critics as unparalleled bursts of intellect. As a rule, their cleverly devised combinations come down to little intellectualistic jokes and marketable design. Nevertheless, they have managed to make the conceptual art of the seventies, which is demanding, difficult to understand, and taxing on the observers' imagination, creditworthy again. The matadors of those days such as Lawrence Weiner, Douglas Huebler, Robert Barry, and Joseph Kosuth are undergoing a revival. Weiner's word sculptures not only adorn Harald Szeeman's exhibition operas, which the master of arrangement performs in ever new productions to the glory of ambitious European cities which expect to gain from it an artistic veneer for their mercantilistic interests; they can also be seen at the stands of the art fairs that continue to multiply. Taking this financially profitable development into account, numerous supraregional newspapers in Europe have added weekly 'Art Market' sections: After turning one round of the second 'Frankfurt Art' (1990) fair, which was devoted to the works of contemporary artists and is geared to 'new investors' on the art market, one of these newspapers sized up the prevalent trend at the onset of the final decade as follows: 'The

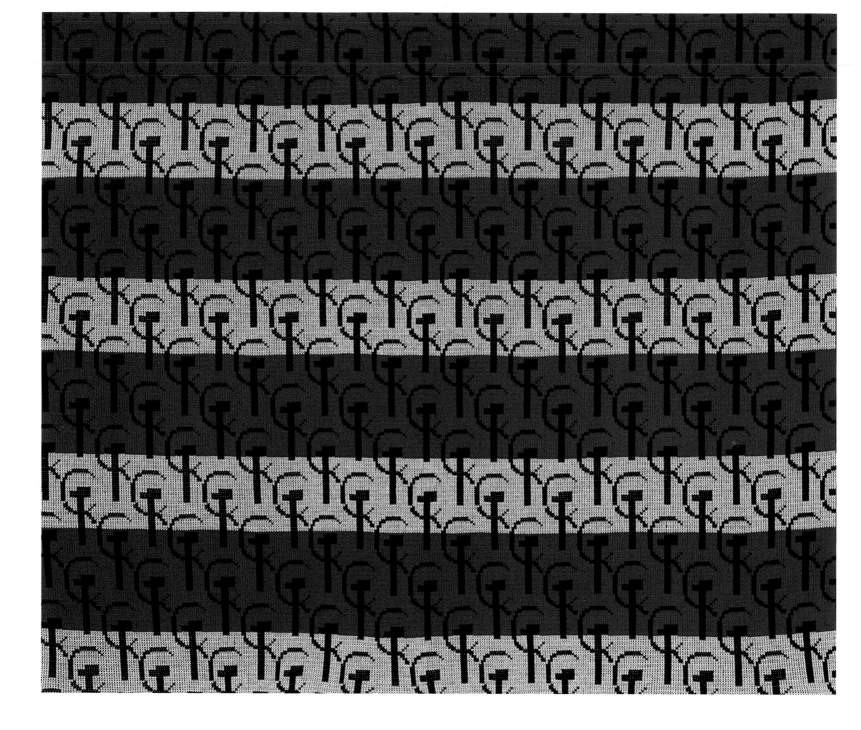

Rosemarie Trockel:
Untitled, 1986
Wool, 51⅛ × 59 in. (130 × 150 cm)
Private collection, Cologne

avant-garde referred back to the recipes of the sixties and seventies, one is thinking in conceptual terms again and working with the minimal means.' The blossoming of ascetic artistic tendencies of late is all the more peculiar against the backdrop of a generally consumeristic attitude among those classes of post-industrial society with purchasing power. Is art perhaps intended to relieve the guilty conscience of its hedonistic clientele, whose collective soul basically still bears the imprint of puritanical structures? Or is it the last bit of evidence for the fact that, really, anything goes?

The weakening of creative power in recent American art is unmistakable at the turn of the century. Important creative fireballs such as Basquiat, Robert Mapplethorpe and Haring died an untimely death of AIDS and left painful gaps behind them. Meanwhile, the artistic vitality of many of the older artists would appear to the intact and they are still able to come up with impressive works of the highest aesthetic standard. Johns, who is at the top of the list on the million-dollar auction circuit, and Stella, who does not rank badly himself on the price lists, have not yet gone to pasture by any means. Their works are captivating, powerful, and instinctually secure, and when it comes to matters of artistic quality, usually leave the young

challengers behind. The price gaps are also still holding: the same names – Johns and Stella, Baselitz, Kiefer, Richter and Poke – have been gracing the 'charts' of the art trade for some time now, surpassed in the financial dimension only by those who, like Beuys and Warhol, are already dead.

Anything is possible, anything goes. As it approaches the new millennium, the contemporary art scene is looking colourful, at times loud, and even impertinent. In Spain and Portugal, East Germany, Poland, Hungary, Czechoslovakia and the Soviet Union, it is staking out new terrain and capturing new sales markets, a fortified European art trade; and while art is convalescing in the smaller countries of Europe such as the Netherlands and Belgium, Switzerland and Austria, art in the United States has grown weary – but despite the prophecies of gloom that cannot be overheard, the stage is still set for expansion. And a German art that has never been stronger since the age of Dürer.

Rosemarie Trockel:
Untitled, 1985
Oil on canvas, 15¾ × 19⅝ in.
(40 × 50 cm) each
Galerie Monika Sprüth, Cologne

Biographical Notes

Georg Baselitz

Jean-Michel Basquiat

Hans Peter Adamski
1947 Born in Kloster Oesede. **1970-1974** Studied at the State Academy of Art in Düsseldorf. Now living in Cologne.

p. 117 Hiroshima, 1981

John Armleder
1948 Born in Geneva. **1966/67** Studied at the Ecole des Beaux Arts, Geneva. Living in Geneva.

p. 190 Untitled, 1987

Elvira Bach
1951 Born in Neuenhain/Taunus, West Germany. **1972-1979** . Studied under Hann Trier at the Academy of Fine Art in Berlin. Now living in Berlin.

p. 119 Untitled, 1985

Ina Barfuss
1949 Born in Lüneburg. **1968-1974** Studied at the Academy of Fine Art in Berlin. Living in Berlin.

p.112 Sacrificial Gift (of the Self to the Id), 1986

Georg Baselitz (Georg Kern)
1938 Born in Deutschbaselitz (Saxony). **1956** Studied painting at the Academy of Fine and Applied Art, East Berlin. **1957-1964** Studied painting under Hann Trier at the Academy of Fine Art in West Berlin. **1983** Professorship at the Academy of Fine Art in West Berlin. **1986** Kaiserring Award of the City of Goslar. Georg Baselitz is now living and working in Berlin and Denneburg.

1963 Solo exhibition at the Galerie Werner & Katz, Berlin. **1972** Kunstmuseum in Basle, documenta 5, Kassel. **1975** 13th Biennial Exhibition São Paolo. **1976** Kunsthalle, Cologne. **1980** Venice Biennial. **1981** A New Spirit in Painting, Royal Academy of Art, London; Westkunst (Western Art), Cologne Exhibition Centre. **1982** documenta 7, Kassel; Zeitgeist, Martin Gropius House, West Berlin. **1984** Stedelijk Museum, Amsterdam, followed by an exhibition at the Dusseldort Exhibition Centre. **1985** Nouvelle Bienniale, Paris, Art in the Federal Republic of Germany, 1945-1985, National Gallery, West Berlin. **1987** Kestner Society, Hanover; Ludwig Museum, Cologne.

p.10 Forward Wind, 1966
p.19 Great Friends, 1965
p.51 E.N. Idol, 1964
p.56 Orange Eater, 1981
p.57 Head of Tears, 1986
p.59 Sliced Head, 1986
p.60/61 45, 1989

Jean-Michel Basquiat
1960 Born in Brooklyn, New York. Died in 1986.

p.151 Cadillac Moon, 1981
p.152 Max Roach, 1984
p.153 Tabac, 1984
p.154/155 Profit I, 1982

Joseph Beuys
1921 Born in Krefeld. **1941** Trained to be a fighter pilot. **1943** Crashed over the Crimea. **1946** Returned from British P.O.W. camps. **1947-1952** Studied sculpture under Josef Enseling and Ewald Mataré at the State Academy of Art in Düsseldorf. **1961** Professorship in sculpture at the State Academy of Art in Düsseldorf. **1972** Dismissed without notice because of his resistance against university entrance restrictions. **1973** Founded the *Free International Academy for Creativity and Inter-Disciplinary Research*. **1975** Honorary professorship of Nova Scotia College of Art, Halifax, Canada. **1978**

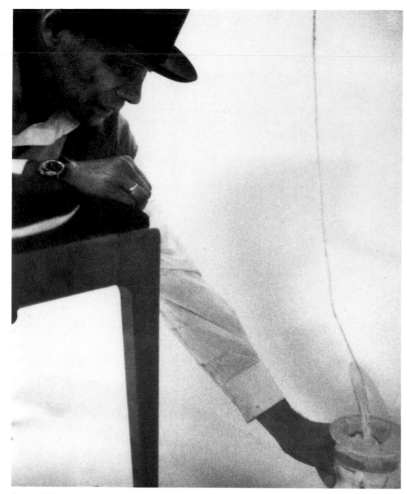

Joseph Beuys

Werner Büttner

Kaiserring Award of the City of Goslar. **1986** Lehmbruck Award of the City of Duisburg. **1986** Died in Oberkassel, near Düsseldorf.
1964 documenta 3, Kassel. **1965** Exhibition at the Schmela Gallery, Düsseldorf. **1968** documenta 4, Kassel. **1971** Moderna Museet, Stockholm. **1972** documenta 5, Kassel. **1976** German Pavilion, Venice Biennial. **1977** documenta 6, Kassel. **1979** 15th Biennial Exhibition, São Paolo. **1979/80** Retrospective exhibition at the Solomon R. Guggenheim Museum, New York. **1980** National Gallery, West Berlin. **1981** Westkunst (Western Art), Cologne Exhibition Centre. **1982** documenta 7, Kassel; Zeitgeist, Martin Gropius House, West Berlin, followed by: **1984** Düsseldorf Exhibition Centre. **1985** Art in the Federal Republic of Germany, 1945-1985, National Gallery, West Berlin; Palazzo Reale, Naples. **1986** Art Society of Rhineland and Westphalia, Düsseldorf. Died in 1986.

p.42 Table with Aggregate, 1958-85
p.43 Grand Piano Yom (Area Yom) 1969
p.44 The End of the 20th Century, 1983
p.45 Fond VII/2, 1985

Ashley Bickerton
1959 Born in Barbados, West Indies. Studied at the California Institute of the Arts, Valencia, California and attended the Whitney Museum's study programme in New York. **1989** Sonnabend Gallery, New York. **1990** Donald Young Gallery, Chicago.

p.8 Tormented Self-Portrait, 1988

Ross Bleckner
1949 Born in New York. **1971-1973** Studied at New York University and California Institute of the Arts, Valencia. M.A. in Fine Arts. Lives in New York.

p.30 Oceans, 1984

Anna Blume
1937 Born in Bork. **1960-1965** Non-examination student at the State Academy of Art in Düsseldorf. Has been working together with Bernhard Johannes Blume on "a lifelong photo novel." Lives in Cologne.

p.176 Kitchen Tantrums, 1986/87

Bernhard Johannes Blume
1937 Born in Dortmund. Trained as a decorative painter and graphic designer. **1960-1965** Non-examination student at the State Academy of Art in Düsseldorf. Best student of Joseph Fassbender. **1967-1971** Studied philosophy and art education in Cologne. Professorship at the Academy of Fine Art in Hamburg. Now living and working in Cologne.
1961 First solo exhibition at Helga Nebelung Gallery, Düsseldorf. **1974** Miracles of Nature, Magers Gallery, Bonn. **1975/76** Exhibition together with Klauke, Marx, Mields, Paeffgen and Prager at the Cologne Art Society. **1977** documenta, Kassel. **1979** Schlaglichter (Highlights), Rheinisches Landesmuseum, Bonn. **1980** Venice Biennial. **1982** Folkwang Museum, Essen, followed by: **1984** Düsseldorf Exhibition Centre. Art After **1945**, National Gallery, Berlin. **1987** Photo Sequences (together with Anna Blume), Kunsthalle, Basle.

p.176 Kitchen Tantrums, 1986/87

Christian Boltanski
1944 Born in Paris, Taught himself. Lives in Paris.
p. 211 Monument, 1986

Peter Bömmels
1951 Born in Frauenberg. **1970-76** Studied sociology, political sciences, and theory of education at Cologne University. Lives in Cologne.

p. 108 Leap from History, 1982

Sandro Chia

Francesco Clemente

Herbert Brandl
1952 Born in Graz, Austria. Studied at the Academy of Applied Art, Vienna. Lives in Vienna.

p. 20 Untitled, 1984/85

Werner Büttner
1954 Born in Jena (East Germany). Studied law in West Berlin. **1976** Founded Union for the Resistance of Contradictory Behaviour together with Albert Oehlen. Lives in Hamburg. **1981** Solo exhibition at Max Hetzler Gallery, Stuttgart. **1982** Twelve Artists from Germany, Kunsthalle, Basle and Boymans van Beunigen Museum, Rotterdam; Zeitgeist, Martin Gropius House, West Berlin; Tendencies 82, Ulm Museum. **1983/84** Modern German Paintings – An Interim Statement, New Gallery at the Joanneum State Museum, Graz, Austria; Villa Stuck Museum, Munich, Rheinisches Landesmuseum, Bonn. **1984** Truth is Work (together with Martin Kippenberger and Albert Oehlen), Folkwang Museum, Essen.

p. 6 Take Care of Your Teeth Like Your Weapons, 1986
p. 130 Brothers with Music, 1984

James Lee Byars
1932 Born in Detroit. Studied at Wayne State University and Meril Palmer School of Psychology in the early sixties. Lives in New York and Venice.

p. 189 The Conscience, 1985

Sandro Chia
1946 Born in Florence. Studied at the Accademia di Belle Arti in Florence. Travelled in Europe and India. Has been officially resident in Rome since 1970. **1980** Apartment in New York. Scholarship to study in Mönchengladbach, West Germany, from September **1980** to August **1981.** Lives and works in New York as well as Ronciglione, near Rome.
1971 First individual exhibition at the Galleria La Salita, Rome. **1973** Italy Two: Art Around '70, Museum of the Philadelphia Civic Centre, Philadel-

phia. **1977** Tenth Paris Biennial, Musée d'Art Moderne de la Ville de Paris. **1979** Arte Cifra, Paul Maenz Gallery, Cologne; XVth Biennial Exhibition, São Paolo; Europe 79, Stuttgart. **1980** Venice Biennial; Seven Young Artists from Italy, Kunsthalle, Basle; Folkwang Museum, Essen; Stedelijk Museum, Amsterdam. **1981** Sperone Westwater Fischer, New York; Bruno Bischofberger Gallery, Zurich; Westkunst (Western Art), Cologne Exhibition Centre; A New Spirit in Painting, Royal Academy of Art, London. **1982** Zeitgeist, Martin Gropius House, West Berlin, documenta 7, Kassel. **1983** Solo exhibition at the Stedelijk Museum, Amsterdam. **1983/84** Pictures (1976–1983), comprehensive touring exhibition of the Kestner Society, Hanover; Staatliche Kunsthalle, Berlin; Musée d'Art Moderne de la Ville de Paris; Mathildenhöhe, Darmstadt; Art Society of Rhineland and Westphalia, Düsseldorf; Museum of Modern Art, Vienna. **1986** Kunsthalle, Bielefeld.

p. 86 Smoker with Yellow Glove, 1980
p. 88 Hand Game, 1981
p. 93 Blue Grotto, 1980
p. 96/97 Incident at the Café Tintoretto, 1982

Francesco Clemente
1952 Born in Naples. **1970** Studied architecture in Rome. **1973/74** Travelled in India and Afghanistan. **1980** First time in New York. Francesco Clemente has been living and working in Rome, Madras and New York.
1971 First solo exhibition at the Galleria Valle Giulia, Rome. **1973** Italy Two, Museum of the Philadelphia Civic Centre. **1975** São Paolo Biennial Exhibition. **1977** Tenth Paris Biennial, Musée d'Art Moderne de la Ville de Paris. **1979** Arte Cifra, Paul Maenz Gallery, Cologne; Europe 79, Stuttgart. **1980** Venice Biennial; Seven Young Artists from Italy, Kunsthalle, Basle; Folkwang Museum, Essen; Stedelijk Museum, Amsterdam. **1981** Westkunst (Western Art), Cologne Exhibition Centre; Sperone Westwater Fischer, New York; Bruno Bischofberger Gallery, Zurich. **1982** documenta 7, Kassel; Zeitgeist, Martin Gropius House, West Berlin. **1983** Recent

Enzo Cucchi

Walter Dahn

European Painting, The Solomon R. Guggenheim Museum, New York. **1984** An International Survey of Recent Painting and Sculpture, The Museum of Modern Art, New York; National Gallery, West Berlin. **1986** Europe/America, Ludwig Museum, Cologne. **1987** The Museum of Contemporary Art, Los Angeles, California (end of a large-scale exhibition tour through America).

p. 98 Alpine Grip, 1987
p. 99 Suonno, 1982
p. 100/101 Tender Lie, 1984

George Condo
1957 Born in New Hampshire. Lives in Paris.

p. 184 Conversation, 1983

Enzo Cucchi
1950 Born in Morro d'Alba, Italy. **1965** Left school and worked for a restorer of paintings in Florence. **1966-1968** Worked as a land surveyor. Enzo Cucchi has been living and working in Ancona and Rome.
1977 Solo exhibition at Incontri Internazionali d'Arte, Rome. **1979** Europe 79, Stuttgart; XVth Biennial, São Paolo. **1980** The Decapitated Hand – A Hundred Drawings from Italy, Kunsthalle, Basle; Folkwang Museum, Essen; Stedelijk Museum, Amsterdam; Venice Biennial. **1981** Westkunst (Western Art), Cologne Exhibition Centre. **1982** documenta 7, Kassel; Zeitgeist, Martin Gropius House, West Berlin; exhibition of drawings at the Kunsthaus, Zurich; Groningen Museum. **1983** Solo exhibition at the Stedelijk Museum, Amsterdam. **1985** Bernd Klüser Gallery, Munich; Kunstmuseum, Düsseldorf. **1986** Retrospective exhibition at Solomon R. Guggenheim Museum, New York; Centre Georges Pompidou, Paris. **1987** Solo exhibition at the Kunsthalle, Bielefeld; State Gallery of Modern Art, Munich; State Gallery at the Lenbach House, Munich; documenta 8, Kassel.

p. 92 Untitled, 1985

p. 94/95 Enchanted City, 1986
p. 103 Uncultivated Landscape, 1983

Walter Dahn
1954 Born in Krefeld. **1971-1977** Studied at the State Academy of Art in Düsseldorf. Joseph Beuys's best student. **1983/84** Lecturer at the State Academy of Art, Düsseldorf. Walter Dahn lives and works in Cologne.
1976 Beuys and His Students, Frankfurt Art Society. **1980** Mülheimer Freiheit and Interesting Pictures from Germany, Paul Maenz Gallery, Cologne. **1982** First solo exhibition at Paul Maenz Gallery; documenta 7, Kassel; Zeitgeist, Martin Gropius House, West Berlin. **1983/84** Modern German Paintings – An Interim Statement, New Gallery at the Joanneum State Museum, Graz, Austria; Villa Stuck Museum, Munich; Rheinisches Landesmuseum, Bonn, followed by: **1984** Düsseldorf Exhibition Centre. **1985** Art in the Federal Republic of Germany, 1945-1985, National Gallery, West Berlin; Photographic Works, Rheinisches Landesmuseum, Bonn. **1986** Paintings (1981-1985), Kunsthalle, Basle; Folkwang Museum, Essen. **1987** Paintings, Sculptures and Drawings (1984-87), Stedelijk van Abbe Museum, Eindhoven.

p. 106 Asthma I, 1982
p. 107 The Victory of Good over Evil (News of H.U.B.), 1986
p. 109 Crystal Morning, 1983
p. 114/115 Self, Twice, 1982

Richard Deacon
1949 Born in Bangor, North Wales. **1974-1977** Studied at the Royal College of Art, London. Lives in London.

p. 209 Two Can Play, 1983

Jiri Georg Dokoupil

Eric Fischl

Martin Disler
1949 Born in Seewen, Switzerland. Lives in Zurich, New York and Harlingen/Holland.

p. 16 Thinking of India, 1982

Jiri Georg Dokoupil
1954 Born in Krnov, Czechoslovakia. **1976-1979** Studied art in Cologne, Frankfurt and New York (Cooper Union, under Hans Haacke). **1983/84** Lecturer at the Academy of Art in Düsseldorf. Lives in Cologne, New York and Tenerife.
1980 Mülheimer Freiheit and Interesting Pictures from Germany, Paul Maenz Gallery, Cologne. **1982** Twelve Artists from Germany, Kunsthalle, Basle and Boymans van Beuningen Museum, Rotterdam; Zeitgeist, Martin Gropius House, West Berlin; documenta 7, Kassel; Venice Biennial. **1983/84** Modern German Paintings – An Interim Statement, New Gallery at the Joanneum State Museum, Graz; Villa Stuck Museum, Munich; Rheinisches Landesmuseum, Bonn. Followed by: **1984** Düsseldorf Exhibition Centre; Dokoupil: Arbeiten (Works)**1981-1984,** Folkwang Museum, Essen. **1985** Museum of Art, Lucerne; Groninger Museum, Groningen; Espace Lyonnais d'Art Contemporain, Lyon. **1986** Sonsbeek 86, Arnhem; Prospect 86, Frankfurt Art Society.

p. 21 In Search of the Twentieth Century Icon, 1983
p. 116 The Studio, 1984

Helmut Federle
1944 Born in Solothurn, Switzerland. **1964-1969** Basle School of Trade and Industry. Lives in Vienna.

p. 191 Three Shapes, Two Crossed, 1985

Rainer Fetting
1949 Born in Wilhelmshaven, West Germany. **1972-1978** Studied at the Academy of Art, Berlin. Lives in Berlin and New York.

p. 110 Man under the Shower IV, 1981/82
p. 134 Phone Call, 1984

Eric Fischl
1948 Born in New York. **1970-1972** Studied at the California Institute of the Arts, Valencia, California. **1974-1978** Lectureship at Nova Scotia College, Halifax, Canada. Lives and works in New York.
1975 First solo exhibition at the Dalhousie Art Gallery, Halifax, Nova Scotia. **1978** Nine Canadian Artists, Kunsthalle, Basle. **1982** Solo exhibitions: Edward Thorp Gallery, New York; University of Colorado Art Galleries, Boulder, Colorado. **1983** Whitney Biennial, Whitney Museum of American Art, New York. **1983/84** Back to the U.S.A., Museum of Art, Lucerne; Rheinisches Landesmuseum, Bonn; Württemberg Art Society, Stuttgart. **1984** Venice Biennial; Aspects of American Contemporary Art, New Gallery, Ludwig Collection, Aachen; Mary Boone Gallery, New York; American Art Since 1970, Whitney Museum of American Art, New York. **1985** Nouvelle Biennale, Paris. **1985/86** Large-scale solo exhibition tour at the Mendel Art Gallery, Saskatoon, Canada; Stedelijk van Abbe Museum, Eindhoven; Kunsthalle, Basle; Institute of Contemporary Art, London; Art Gallery of Ontario, Toronto, Canada; Museum of Contemporary Art, Chicago; The Broida Museum, New York. **1986** Europe/America, Ludwig Museum, Cologne. **1987** documenta 8, Kassel.

p. 144 Birthday Boy, 1983
Front cover. *p. 145* Bad Boy, 1981
p. 146 Sleepwalker, 1979
p. 147 Best Western, 1983
p. 148/149 Cargo Cults, 1984

Günther Förg

Gilbert & George

Günther Förg
1952 Born in Füssen, West Germany. **1973-1979** Studied at the Academy of Fine Art in Munich. Lives in Munich and Cologne.

p. 166 Lyngotte III, 1989
p. 181 Exhibition Max Hetzler Gallery, Cologne, Oct. 1986
p. 186 Fall II, 1984

Gérard Garouste
1946 Born in Paris. Lives in Marcilly-sur-Eure.

p. 102 Columbia, 1981

Isa Genzken
1948 Born in Bad Oldesloe, West Germany. **1973-1977** Studied at the State Academy of Art in Düsseldorf. Living in Cologne.

p. 212 Corridor, 1986

Gilbert & George
Gilbert: **1943** Born in the Dolomite Mountains in Southern Tyrol. George: **1942** Born in Totnes, Devonshire.
1967 First meeting of the two artists while they were both studying at St. Martin's Art School, London. Since **1968** they have been working together as *Living Sculptures*, living in London. **1971** Large-scale joint exhibition at Whitechapel Art Gallery, London; Stedelijk Museum, Amsterdam; Art Society of the Rhineland and Westphalia, Düsseldorf. **1972** documenta 5, Kassel. **1976** Ileana Sonnabend Gallery, New York. **1977** documenta 6, Kassel; Venice Biennial. **1980**
Photo-Pieces 1971-1980, Stedelijk van Abbe Museum, Eindhoven. **1981** Kunsthalle, Düsseldorf; Kunsthalle, Berne; Centre Georges Pompidou, Paris. **1981** Westkunst (Western Art), Cologne Exhibition Centre. **1982** Zeitgeist, Martin Gropius House, West Berlin; documenta 7, Kassel. **1986** Pictures 1982-1985 , Kunsthalle, Basle.

p. 188 I, 1987

Robert Gober
1954 Born in Wallingford, Connecticut. Studied at the Tyler School of Art in Rom and at Middlebury College in Vermont. **1988** Galerie Max Hetzler, Cologne. **1989** Paula Cooper Gallery, New York.

p. 206 Three Urinals, 1988
p. 207 Untitled, 1985–1987

Leon Golub
1922 Born in Chicago. **1940-1942** Studied history of art at the University of Chicago. **1946-1959** Studied painting at the School of Art Institute, Chicago. Has held a John C. van Dyck lectureship of Visual Arts at Rutgers University, New Brunswick, New Jersey, since **1983** . Lives in New York.

p. 216 Mercenaries VI, 1987

Asta Gröting
1961 Born in Düsseldorf. **1989** Galerie Isabella Kaprzak, Stuttgart. Kunstverein für die Rheinlande und Westfalen, Düsseldorf.

p. 214 The Happy Marriage, 1989

Peter Halley
1953 Born in New York. Studied at Yale University, New Haven and at the University of New Orleans. **1989** Sonnabend Gallery, New York. Institute of Contemporary Art, London.

p. 163 Black Cell with Conduit Twice, 1988

Keith Haring
1958 Born in Kutztown, Pennsylvania. Died in 1990. **1980** Times Square Show, New York. **1981** Solo exhibition in Westbeth Painters Space, New York. **1982** documenta 7, Kassel; Rotterdam Arts Council, Rotterdam. **1983** Biennial, Whitney Museum of American Art, New York. **1983/84** Back to the U.S.A, Art Museum, Lucerne; Rheinisches Landesmuseum, Bonn;

Keith Haring

Karl Horst Hödicke

Württemberg Art Society, Stuttgart. **1984** Solo exhibition at Paul Maenz Gallery, Cologne. **1986** Large-scale solo exhibition at the Stedelijk Museum, Amsterdam. **1987** Sculpture Projects, Münster.

p. 31 Exhibition from 3rd to 30th May 1984 at Paul Maenz Gallery
p. 32 Untitled, April 1984
p. 33 Untitled, 12th April 1984

Georg Herold
1947 Born in Jena, East Germany. Lives in Cologne.

p. 129 Beluga, 1989

Antonius Höckelmann
1937 Born in Oelde, West Germany. **1957-1961** Studied under Prof. Karl Hartung at the Academy of Fine Art in Berlin. Lives in Cologne.

p. 219 The Newspaper Reader, 1985/87

Karl Horst Hödicke
1938 Born in Nuremberg. **1959** Studied under Fred Thieler at the Academy of Fine Art in Berlin. **1974** Professorship at the Academy of Fine Art, Berlin. Lives in Berlin.

p. 17 Black Gobi, 1982

Jenny Holzer
1950 Born in Gallipolis, Ohio. Studied at Rhode Island School of Design. Lives in New York.

p. 183 From the Survival Series, 1987

Thomas Huber
1955 Born in Zurich. Studied at the School of Art and Design, Basle, the

Royal College of Art, London, and under Fritz Schwegler at the State Academy of Art, Düsseldorf. Lives in Düsseldorf.

p. 185 Design for a Building-Site Poster, 1986

Jörg Immendorff
1945 Born in Bleckede, near Lüneburg, West Germany. **1963/64** Studied theatrical art under Theo Otto at the State Academy of Art in Düsseldorf. **1964** Changed over to Joseph Beuys's classes. **1981** On sabbatical at the Royal School of Art, Stockholm. **1982-1985** Guest lecturer at the Academy of Fine Art, Hamburg, the Academy of Art, Trondheim and Cologne Polytechnic. Now living and working in Düsseldorf.
1965 Solo exhibition at Schmela Gallery, Düsseldorf. **1972** documenta 5, Kassel. **1975** Here and Now - What Needs Doing, Westphalian Art Society, Münster. **1976** Venice Biennial. **1979** Café Deutschland, Museum of Art, Basle. **1980** Les Nouveaux Fauves – The New Savages, New Gallery, Ludwig Collection, Aachen; Venice Biennial. **1981** Westkunst (Western Art), Cologne Exhibition Centre. **1982** documenta 7, Kassel; Zeitgeist, Martin Gropius House, West Berlin. **1984** Kunsthalle, Hamburg; followed by: Düsseldorf Exhibition Centre. **1985** Art in the Federal Republic of Germany 1945-1985, National Gallery, West Berlin. **1986** Europe/America, Ludwig Museum, Cologne.

p. 18 And Now the 38th Party Congress, 1983
p. 63 Pot, 1985
p. 68 Ambassador on Grass, 1967

Anish Kapoor
1954 Born in Bombay. Lives in London.

p. 208 1000 Names, 1981

Mike Kelley
1954 Born in Detroit, Michigan. Studied at the University of Michigan, Ann

Jörg Immendorff

Anselm Kiefer

Arbor and the California Institute of the Arts, Valencia. Lives in Los Angeles. **1989** Rosamund Felsen Gallery, Los Angeles. Jablonka Galerie, Cologne. **1990** Metro Pictures, New York.

p. 164/165 Pansy Metal Covered Hoof, 1989

Hubert Kiecol
1950 Born in Bremen. Studied at the Academy of Fine Art, Hamburg. Lives in Cologne.

p. 200 Clinker Sculptures, 1983
p. 201 Column Lying on Its Side, 1987

Anselm Kiefer
1945 Born in Donaueschingen, Bavaria, West Germany. **1966-1968** Learnt to paint under Peter Dreher in Freiburg. **1969** Studied under Horst Antes at the Academy of Art, Karlsruhe. **1970-1972** Studied under Joseph Beuys at the Academy of Art, Düsseldorf. Anselm Kiefer is now living in Hornbach and working in Buchen/Odenwald.
1969 First solo exhibition at the Kaiserplatz Gallery, Karlsruhe. **1973** 14 × 14, State Art Gallery, Baden-Baden. **1975** Project Sea Lion, Michael Werner Gallery, Cologne. **1977** Bonn Art Society at the Rheinisches Landesmuseum, Bonn; documenta 6, Kassel. **1981** A New Spirit in Painting, Royal Academy of Art, London; Westkunst (Western Art), Cologne Exhibition Centre. **1982** documenta 7, Kassel; Zeitgeist, Martin Gropius House, West Berlin. **1984** Kunsthalle, Düsseldorf; ARC/Musée d'Art Moderne de la Ville de Paris; The Israel Museum, Jerusalem; followed by: Düsseldorf Exhibition Centre. **1985** German Twentieth Century Art, Painting and Sculpture 1905-1985, Royal Academy of Art, London; Art in the Federal Republic of Germany 1945-1985, National Gallery, West Berlin. **1986/87** Stedelijk Museum, Amsterdam. **1987** documenta 8, Kassel.

p. 14 Quaternity, 1973
p. 50 The Stairs, 1982/83

p. 52 Ways of the World's Wisdom – The Battle of the Teutoburg Forest, 1978
p. 53 To the Unknown Painter, 1982
p. 54 Painting the Burnt Earth, 1974
p. 55 Sulamith, 1983

Martin Kippenberger
1953 Born in Dortmund. **1972** Enrolled at the Academy of Fine Art, Hamburg. **1978** Founded Kippenberger's Office, Berlin. Now living and working in Cologne.
1977 Chimeras (together with Ina Barfuss and Thomas Wachweger), Hamburg. **1981** Solo exhibition at the Petersen Gallery, Berlin; Rundschau Deutschland I, Lothringer Strasse, Munich. **1982** Tendencies 82, Ulm Museum. **1983** Song of Joy (with Wilhelm Schürmann), Neue Gallerie, Ludwig Collection, Aachen. **1983/74** Modern German Paintings – An Interim Statement, New Gallery at the Joanneum State Museum, Graz; Villa Stuck Museum, Munich; Rheinisches Landesmuseum, Bonn. **1984** Truth is Work (together with Werner Büttner and Albert Oehlen). Folkwang Museum, Essen; followed by Düsseldorf Exhibition Centre. **1985** Art in the Federal Republic of Germany, 1945-1985, National Gallery, West Berlin; solo exhibition at Max Hetzler Gallery, Cologne, Erhard Klein Gallery, Bonn. **1986** Modern German Art from the Ludwig Collection, Aachen; Metternich House, Koblenz. **1987** BERLINART 1961-1987, The Museum of Modern Art, New York.

p. 39 War Wicked, 1983
p. 120/121 Buggered for Ideas, 1982/83
p. 122 Dialogue with the Young, 1981
p. 123 Pleasant Communist Girl, 1983
p. 123 Not Knowing Why, But Knowing What For, 1984
Backcover: Sozialkistentransporter, 1989

Martin Kippenberger

Jürgen Klauke

Per Kirkeby
1938 Born in Copenhagen. Lives in Copenhagen, Læso and Karlsruhe.

p. 23 Winter VI, 1986

Jürgen Klauke
1943 Born in Kliding, near Cochem (Moselle). **1961-1965** Studied graphic design at Cologne Polytechnic. **1975-79** Lecturer in graphic design at Cologne Polytechnic. Guest lecturer at the Academy of Fine Art, Hamburg, as well as the Academies of Art in Munich and Kassel. Now living and working in Cologne and Kassel.
1973 Rheinisches Landesmuseum, Bonn. **1975** Six Artists from Cologne, Cologne Art Society, Cologne. **1977** documenta 6, Kassel. **1979** Highlights, Rheinisches Landesmuseum, Bonn; Masculine-Feminine, New Gallery at the Joanneum State Museum, Graz. **1980** Venice Biennial. **1981** Westkunst (Western Art), Cologne Exhibition Centre; Jürgen Klauke – Formalization of Boredom, Museum of Art, Lucerne; Rheinisches Landesmuseum, Bonn; New Gallery at the Joanneum State Museum, Graz. **1982-1984** Klein Gallery, Bonn. **1985** Art in the Federal Republic of Germany, 1945-1985, National Gallery, West Berlin. **1986** Androgyne, New Berlin Art Society, West Berlin. **1986/87** Retrospective exhibitions of the Baden Art Society (Karlsruhe), Kunsthalle (Hamburg), Boymans van Beunigen Museum (Rotterdam) and the Ludwig Museum (Cologne). **1987** documenta 8, Kassel.

p. 168 Home Game, 1985
p. 170 From: Shadow Pictures, 1984

Astrid Klein
1951 Born in Cologne. **1973-1977** Studied at Cologne Polytechnic. Lives in Cologne.

p. 169 Cerebral Somersault, 1984

Bernd Koberling
1938 Born in Berlin. **1958-1960** Studied at the Academy of Fine Art in Berlin. Has been professor at the same university since **1981**. Lives in Hamburg and Berlin.

p. 34 Big Breeder, 1981

Jeff Koons
1955 Born in York, Pennsylvania. Lives in New York.

p. 2 Ushering the Banality, 1988
p. 27 Louis (XIV), 1986
p. 195 Two Balls 50/50 Tank, 1985
p. 195 New Hoover Convertibles, 1981-1987

Barbara Kruger
1945 Born in Newark, New Jersey. **1965** Studied at Syracuse University and at Parsons School of Design, New York, in **1966** . Lives in New York.

p. 180 Installation, 1987

Milan Kunc
1944 Born in Prague. Lives in Cologne.

p. 179 The World is Unfathomable, 1986

Robert Kushner
1949 Born in Pasadena, California. **1971** Graduated from the University of California in San Diego. Living in New York.

p. 68 Sail Away, 1983

Robert Longo

Markus Lüpertz

Thomas Lanigan-Schmidt
1948 Born in Elizabeth, New Jersey. Lives in New York.

p. 71 The Preying Hands, 1983

Robert Longo
1953 Born in Brooklyn, New York. **1975** Graduated in art at the State University College, Buffalo, New York.Lives in New York.

p. 160 Now Everybody, 1982-83
p. 161 Corporate Wars: Wall of Influence, 1982

Nino Longobardi
1953 Born in Naples. Lives in Naples.

p. 24 Untitled, 1986
p. 25 Untitled, 1979

Markus Lüpertz
1941 Born in Liberec, Czechoslovakia. **1956-1961** Studied at the School of Art and Design in Krefeld and the State Academy of Art in Düsseldorf. **1986** Professorship at the State Academy of Art, Düsseldorf. Lives in Düsseldorf and Berlin.

p. 22 Dithyrambe, 1964
p. 64 Ghosts in the Spaces: Eurystheus II, 1987
p. 65 Melon Mathematics XXIII, 1984/85

Kim MacConnel
1947 Born in Oklahoma City, Oklahoma. **1969** Studied at the University of California in San Diego. Lives in Encinitas, California.

p. 70 Paintings and Occasional Chairs, 1984

Karl Marx
1929 Born in Cologne. Head of the Art and Design Department at Cologne Polytechnic. Lives in Cologne.

p. 217 Man with Shadow. Self-Portrait, 1982

Ian McKeever
1946 Born in Withernsea, Yorkshire. Studied at Avery Hill College of Education, London. Lives in London.

p. 28 Crossing, 1986

Gerhard Merz
1947 Born in Mannendorf, Bavaria. **1969-1973** Studied at the Academy of Art, Munich. Lives in Munich.

p. 187 Victory of the Sun MCMLXXXVII, 1987

Helmut Middendorf
1953 Born in Dinklage, West Germany. **1971-1979** Studied painting at the Academy of Art, Berlin. **1977** Co-founder of the Galerie am Moritzplatz. **1979** Lectureship in experimental films at the Academy of Art, Berlin. **1980** Scholarship of the German Academic Exchange Service to study in New York. Lives in Berlin.

p. 118 Singer IV, 1981
p. 132 Aeroplane Dream, 1982

Reinhard Mucha
1950 Born in Düsseldorf. Studied at the State Academy of Art, Düsseldorf. **1981** Will Grohmann Scholarship. Lives in Düsseldorf.

p. 198 Wind and Towers, Too High, 1982
p. 199 The Fundamental Problem in the Figures of Baroque Architecture, 1985

Reinhard Mucha

Albert Oehlen

Albert Oehlen
1954 Born in Krefeld. **1976** Founded Union for the Resistance of Contradictory Behaviour together with Werner Büttner. Lives and works in Düsseldorf

1980 Mülheimer Freiheit and Interesting Pictures from Germany, Paul Maenz Gallery, Cologne. **1981** First solo exhibition at Max Hetzler Gallery, Stuttgart, and Philomene Magers Gallery, Bonn; Anti-Pictures, Baden Art Society, Karlsruhe. **1982** Boymans von Beuningen Museum, Rotterdam. **1983** Rudolf Zwirner Gallery, Cologne. **1983/84** Modern German Paintings – An Interim Statement, New Gallery at the Joanneum State Museum, Graz; Rheinisches Landesmuseum, Bonn. **1984** Truth is Work, Folkwang Museum, Essen; followed by: Düsseldorf Exhibition Centre. **1985** 7000 Oaks, Kunsthalle Bielefeld, Kunsthalle Tübingen. **1986** Modern German Art from the Ludwig Collection, Aachen. **1987** Kunsthalle, Zurich.

p. 124 By the Tree, 1984
p. 125 Untitled, 1982
p. 126/127 Not Free But Randy, 1983

Markus Oehlen
1956 Born in Krefeld. **1976-1981** Studied at the State Academy of Art in Düsseldorf. Lives in Hamburg.

p. 113 Landscape, 1987

Julian Opie
1958 Born in London. **1979-1982** Student at the Goldsmith School of Art, London. Lives in London.

p. 194 Oxo, 1984
p. 194 Untitled (Large Pile of Washing-Up), 1985

C.O. Paeffgen
1933 Born in Cologne. Lives in Cologne.

p. 218 Untitled (Queen), 1972

Mimmo Paladino
1948 Born in Paduli, Italy. Lives in Milan and Paduli. **1977** Solo exhibition at the Galleria Lucio Amelio, Naples. **1979** Arte Cifra, Paul Maenz Gallery, Cologne. **1980** Solo exhibitions at the Kunsthalle (Basel), Folkwang Museum (Essen), Stedelijk Museum (Amsterdam), Venice Biennial. **1981** A New Spirit in Painting. Royal Academy of Art, London; Westkunst (Western Art), Cologne Exhibition Centre. **1982** documenta 7, Kassel; Zeitgeist, Martin Gropius House, West Berlin. **1983** Sperone Westwater Gallery, New York. **1985** Solo exhibition at the City Gallery at the Lenbach House, Munich; Nouvelle Biennale, Paris.

p. 90/91 Untitled, 1982
p. 104 Stagnant Water, 1981

A.R. Penck (Ralf Winkler)
1939 Born in Dresden. Taught himself to paint, write and produce films. Lives in London.

p. 11 Untitled, 1966
p. 13 Incident in N.Y. 3, 1983
p. 15 Standpoint, 1971
p. 66 Looking Back at the Quiet Bay, 1977
p. 67 N – Complex, 1976

Sigmar Polke
1941 Born in Oels (Lower Silesia, now part of Poland). **1961-1967** Studied under K.H. Götz and Gerhard Hoehme at the State Academy of Art in Düsseldorf. **1970-1971** Guest lecturer at the Academy of Fine Art, Ham-

Mimmo Paladino

A.R. Penck

burg. **1977** Professorship at same academy. **1982** Will Grohmann Award. **1984** Kurt Schwitters Award. **1985** Lichtwark Award, Hamburg. **1986** Golden Lion Award at the Venice Biennial. Lives and works in Cologne.
1963 Exhibition of the furniture company, Berges. Deomonstration for Capitalist Realism, Düsseldorf (together with K. Lueg and G. Richter). **1968** Museum of Art, Lucerne. **1972** documenta 5, Kassel. **1973** Franz Liszt Enjoys Coming to Watch T.V. at My Place, Westphalian Art Society, Münster. **1974** Spot the Fake, City Museum of Art, Bonn; Project, Cologne Exhibition Centre. **1975** 13th Biennial, São Paolo. **1979** Cologne Art Society, Cologne; Highlights, Rheinisches Landesmuseum, Bonn; **1981** A New Spirit in Painting, Royal Academy of Art, London; Westkunst (Western Art), Cologne Exhibition Centre. **1982** documenta 7, Kassel; Zeitgeist, Martin Gropius House, West Berlin. **1983** It's Always Been Like This / We've Never Done It Like That / What If Everyone Did That? - Boymans van Beuningen Museum, Rotterdam. **1984** City Museum of Art, Bonn; followed by: Düsseldorf Exhibition Centre; Kunsthaus Zurich. **1985** Art in the Federal Republic of Germany, 1945-1985, National Gallery, West Berlin. **1986** Venice Biennial; Positions – Paintings from the Federal Republic of Germany, East Berlin, Dresden, Hanover.

Richard Prince
1949 Born in the Panama Canal Zone, lives in New York. **1988** Galerie Jablonka, Cologne. **1989** Daniel Weinberg Gallery, Los Angels. IVAM Centre del Carme, Valencia.

Gerhard Richter
1932 Born in Dresden (East Germany). **1951-1956** Studied at the Academy of Art in Dresden. **1961** Moved to Düsseldorf, West Germany. **1961-1963** Studied under K.O. Götz at the State Academy of Art in Düsseldorf. **1967** Guest lecturer at the Academy of Fine Art, Hamburg. From **1971** professor at the State Academy of Art, Düsseldorf. **1978** On sabbatical at the College of Art in Halifax, Canada. **1981** Arnold Bode Award, Kassel. **1985** Oskar Kokoschka Award, Vienna. Lives and works in Cologne.
1961 First solo exhibition at the Heiner Friedrich Gallery, Munich. **1969** Counter-Traffic, Aachen. **1972** documenta 5, Kassel; Venice Biennial. **1977** documenta 6, Kassel; Centre Georges Pompidou, Paris. **1980** German Pavilion, Venice Biennial. **1981** A New Spirit in Painting, Royal Academy of Art, London; Westkunst (Western Art), Cologne Exhibition Centre. **1982** documenta 7, Kassel. **1984** followed by Düsseldorf Exhibition Centre. **1985** La Nouvelle Biennale, Paris; Art in the Federal Republic of Germany, 1945-1985. National Gallery, West Berlin. **1986** Retrospectives at the Kunsthalle in Düsseldorf, the National Gallery (West Berlin), the Kunsthalle in Berne and the Museum of Modern Art in Vienna; Positions, Paintings from the Federal Republic of West Germany, East Berlin and Dresden (East Germany) as well as Hanover. **1987** documenta 8, Kassel.

Susan Rothenberg
1945 Born in Buffalo, New York. **1966-1967** Studied at Cornell University, George Washington University and Corcoran Museum School, Washington. Lives in New York.

Sigmar Polke

Gerhard Richter

Ulrich Rückriem
1938 Born in Düsseldorf. **1959** Trained at the Dombauhütte in Cologne. **1975-1984** Professorship at the Academy of Art in Hamburg. **1984** Professorship at the State Academy of Art in Düsseldorf. Lives in Cologne.

p. 202 Pillar, since 1968
p. 203 From a four-part interior installation, 1986
p. 203 Untitled, 1986

Thomas Ruff
1958 Born in Zell am Hammersbach. Lives in Düsseldorf. Studied at the State Academy of Art in Düsseldorf. **1989** 303 Gallery, New York. Galerie Johnen & Schöttle, Cologne. **1990** Kunstmuseum, Bonn

p. 178 Stars 01 h 55–30°, 1990

David Salle
1952 Born in Norman, Oklahoma. **1975** Graduated from the California Institute of the Arts, Valencia. Lives and works in New York.
1975 Solo exhibition at the Claire S. Copley Gallery, Los Angeles. **1976** Foundation Corps de Garde, Groningen. **1977** Locations, Seriaal Gallery, Amsterdam. **1980** l'Amérique aux Indépendants, Grand Palais, Paris. **1981** Westkunst (Western Art), Cologne Exhibition Centre; Mary Boone Gallery, New York. **1982** Avanguardia-Transavanguardia, Muro Aureliane, Rome; documenta 7, Kassel; Zeitgeist, Martin Gropius House, West Berlin. **1983** Solo exhibition at the Boymans van Beuningen Museum, Rotterdam. **1983/84** Back to the U.S.A., Lucerne Art Museum; Rheinisches Landesmuseum, Bonn; Württemberg Art Society, Stuttgart. **1985** Nouvelle Biennale, Paris. **1986** Whitney Museum of American Art, New York.

p. 136 Dual Aspect Picture, 1986
p. 138 Untitled, 1984

p. 139 Untitled, 1984
p. 140 Saltimbanques, 1986
p. 141 Making the Bed, 1985
p. 142/143 Muscular Paper, 1985

Salomé
1954 Born in Karlsruhe. **1974-1980** Studied at the Academy of Art, Berlin. Lives in Berlin.

p. 111 Spirit of the Time IV, 1982

Salvo (Salvatore Mangione)
1947 Born in Leonforte, near Enna, Italy. Lives in Turin.

p. 105 Eight Books, 1983

Kenny Scharf
1958 Born in Los Angeles. Lives in New York.

p. 69 Jungle Jism, 1985

Julian Schnabel
1951 Born in New York. **1969-1973** Studied at Houston University, Texas. **1973-1974** Studied at Whitney Museum of American Art, New York. **1978** Trips to Spain, Italy and Germany. Lives and works in New York.
1978 First European solo exhibition at the December Gallery, Düsseldorf. **1979** Mary Boon Gallery, New York. **1980** Venice Biennial. **1981** A New Spirit in Painting, Royal Academy of Arts, London; Westkunst (Western Art), Cologne Exhibition Centre. **1982** First large-scale museum exhibition at the Stedelijk Museum, Amsterdam; Venice Biennial; Zeitgeist, Martin Gropius Building, West Berlin. **1983/84** Back to the U.S.A., Museum of Art, Lucerne; Rheinisches Landesmuseum, Bonn; Württemberg Art Soci-

Ulrich Rückriem

David Salle

ety, Stuttgart. **1984** *Rose 84*, Dublin; La Grande Parade, Stedelijk Museum, Amsterdam. **1985** Nouvelle Biennale, Paris. **1986** Europe/America, Ludwig Museum, Cologne. **1986/87** Large-scale solo exhibition at the Whitechapel Art Gallery, London, the Centre Georges Pompidou, Paris, the Städtische Kunsthalle, Düsseldorf, and the Whitney Museum of American Art, New York.

p. 156 The Student of Prague, 1983
p. 157 The Sea, 1981
p. 158 The Return from the Hospital, 1982
p. 159 The Dancers (for Pasolini), 1977/78

Rob Scholte
1958 Born in Amsterdam. Lives in Amsterdam.

p. 172 Two Lesbians Mocking, 1983
p. 172 The Scream, 1985

Andreas Schulze
1955 Born in Hanover. **1976-1983** Studied at Kassel University and the State Academy of Art in Düsseldorf. Lives in Cologne.

p. 38 Untitled, 1985
p. 133 Curtain, 1984

Richard Serra
1939 Born in San Francisco. **1961-1965** Studied at the University of California and Yale University, New Haven. Lives in New York and Cape Breton/Nova Scotia, Canada.

p. 212 Street Level, 1987
p. 213 Terminal, 1976/77

Cindy Sherman
1954 Born in Glen Ridge, New Jersey. **1976** B.A. in Photography at State University College, Buffalo, New York. Lives and works in New York.
1976 First solo exhibition at Hallwall's, Buffalo, New York. **1980** Contemporary Art Museum, Houston. **1981** Metro Pictures, New York; Autoportraits, Centre Georges Pompidou, Paris. **1982** Lichtbildnisse (Photographs) – The Portrait in Photography, Rheinisches Landesmuseum; Venice Biennial; documenta 7, Kassel; large-scale solo exhibition at the Stedelijk Museum, Amsterdam (European exhibition tour). **1983/84** Back to the U.S.A. Exhibition, Lucerne Museum of Art; Rheinisches Landesmuseum, Bonn; Württemberg Art Society, Stuttgart; **1984** Monika Sprüth Gallery, Cologne. **1985** Kunst im Eigen-Sinn (Eccentric Art/Art in the Real Sense of the Word), Museum of Modern Art, Vienna; solo exhibition at the Westphalian Art Society, Münster.

p. 171 Untitled, 1985
p. 171 Untitled, 1985
p. 175 Untitled, 1985

Katharina Sieverding
1944 Born in Prague. **1962-1974** Studied at the Academy of Fine Art in Hamburg and the State Academy of Art in Düsseldorf. Lives in Düsseldorf.

p. 177 Continental Nucleus III/XXVI, 1986

Haim Steinbach
1944 Born in Israel. Lives in New York.

p. 197 Untitled, 1987

Frank Stella
1936 Born in Malden, Mass. **1950-1954** Studied painting at the Philips Academy in Andover, Mass. **1954-1958** Princeton University, New Jersey.

Julian Schnabel

Cindy Sherman

1960/61 Travelled around Europe. Lives in New York.
1960 First solo exhibition at Leo Castelli's in New York. **1964** , **1968** and **1972** Venice Biennial. **1968** and **1977** documenta in Kassel.

p. 204 Sinicrli Variation II, 1968
p. 205 Corpo senza l'anima, 1987

Stefan Szczesny
1951 Born in Munich. **1969-1975** Studied at the Academy of Fine Art in Munich. Lives in Cologne.

p. 35 Bathers in the Snow, 1984

Philip Taaffe
1955 Born in New Jersey. Lives in New York.

p. 192 Untitled (Midnight Blue), 1985
p. 193 Nativity (Red White), 1986

Henk Tas
1949 Born in Rotterdam. **1966-1971** Studied at the Academy of Fine Art, Rotterdam. Lives in Rotterdam.

p. 173 Sacred Cow, 1986

Rosemarie Trockel
1952 Born in Schwerte, West Germany. **1974-1978** Studied painting at Cologne Polytechnic. Lives and works in Cologne.
1983 First solo exhibition at Monika Sprüth Gallery, Cologne, Philomene Magers Gallery, Bonn. **1984** Kunstlandschaft BRD (Art Scenery West Germany), Lübeck Art Society; Bella Figura, Lehmbruck Museum, Duisburg. **1985** First large-scale museum exhibition at the Rheinisches Landesmuseum, Bonn; Kunst mit Eigen-Sinn (Eccentric Art/Art in the Real Sense

of the Word), Museum of Modern Art, Vienna; Synonyms of Sculpture, trigon 1985; New Gallery at the Joanneum State Museum, Graz. **1986** Sonsbeek 86, Arnhem; The Sixth Biennial of Sydney. **1987** Wechselströme (Alternating Currents), Bonn Art Society; Art from Europe, Tate Gallery, London, Similia/Dissimilia, Kunsthalle, Düsseldorf.

p. 220 Untitled, 1986
p. 221 Untitled, 1985

Meyer Vaisman
1960 Born in Caracas, Venezuela. Lives in New York.
p. 210 Four Small Fillers, 1987

Thomas Wachweger
1943 Born in Breslau, Silesia (now Wroclaw, Poland). **1963-1970** Studied at the Academy of Fine Art in Hamburg. Lives in Berlin.

p. 112 Evacuation Plan, 1986

Jeff Wall
1946 Born in Vancouver. Studied at the University of British Columbia. **1989** Galerie Johnen & Schöttle, Cologne. Marian Goodman Gallery, New York.

p. 182 The Drain, 1989

Andy Warhol
1928 Born in Pittsburgh, Pennsylvania. **1945-1949** Studied history of art, sociology and psychology at the Carnegie Institute of Technology, Pittsburgh. **1949** Moved to New York. Commercial artist for *Vogue* and *Harper's Bazaar*. Since **1960** freelance artist. **1962** Opening of *The Factory*. **1963** first films. Editor of *Interview*. Died in New York in **1987** .
1952 First solo exhibition at the Hugo Gallery, New York. **1964** Leo Castelli

Rosemarie Trockel

Andy Warhol

Gallery, New York; Pop Art, Stedelijk Museum, Amsterdam. **1966** Institute of Contemporary Art, Boston; The Photographic Image, Solomon R. Guggenheim Museum, New York. **1968** Stedelijk Museum, Amsterdam; documenta 4, Kassel. **1969** National Gallery, West Berlin. **1974** Retrospectives in Tokyo. **1976** Württemberg Art Society, Stuttgart. **1977** documenta 6, Kassel. **1978** Kunsthaus, Zurich; Venice Biennial. **1980** Venice Biennial. **1981** Kestner Society, Hanover; A New Spirit in Painting, Royal Academy of Art, London. Westkunst (Western Art), Cologne Exhibition Centre. **1982** Zeitgeist, Martin Gropius House, West Berlin; documenta 7, Kassel. **1984** Légendes, Musée d'Art Contemporain, Bordeaux. **1986** Europe/America, Ludwig Museum, Cologne. Died in **1987.**

p. 12 Do It Yourself (Seascape)
p. 40 Portrait of Joseph Beuys, 1980
p. 41 Campbell's Soup Can II, 1968
p. 46 Marilyn Twice, 1962
p. 46 Single Elvis, 1964
p. 48 Twenty Jackies, 1964
p. 49 Last Supper, 1986

William Wegman
1943 Born in Holyoke, Massachusetts. Studied at the Massachusetts College of Art, Boston and the University of Illinois, Urbana. Lives in New York.

p. 174 Snap and Chanel, 1982

Franz West
1946 Born in Vienna. Lives in Vienna.

p. 215 Isomorphism, 1986

Bill Woodrow
1948 Born near Henley-on-Thames. Lives in London.

p. 196 Still Waters, 1985

Bernd Zimmer
1948 Born in Planegg, near Munich. Lives in Polling and Berlin.

p. 135 Far – Near, 1985